Ken Oliver
The Benign Bishop

Ken Oliver
The Benign Bishop

Dan Buglass

MARLBOROUGH/PUNCHESTOWN

MARLBOROUGH BOOKS
Unit 22, Cheney Manor, Swindon, SN2 2PJ

c/o 9 Queen Street, Melbourne 3000, Victoria, Australia

PUNCHESTOWN BOOKS
4 Arran Quay, Dublin 7

First published 1994

Typesetting and Origination: Capital City, Swindon
Dustwrapper Design: Ron Stephens

There is a special edition of this book available, limited to 55 copies
of which 50 are for sale – bound in quarter leather, double signed
and numbered. ISBN 1-873919 25 5.

ISBN 1-873919 - 15 8 Marlborough
ISBN 1-873920 - 10 5 Punchestown

Printed in Great Britain by BPCC Wheatons Ltd, Exeter

CONTENTS

* with Rupert Collens
** by Rupert Collens

FOREWORDS

From Harry Beeby
Chairman & Managing Director, Doncaster Bloodstock Sales Ltd.
I was introduced to Kenneth Oliver - The Bishop - at the Schweppes Gold Trophy Meeting at Newbury in February 1964 by his lifelong friend and the joint-founder of Doncaster Bloodstock Sales, the late Willie Stephenson.

After a couple of drinks in the Members Bar, I found myself agreeing to visit Hawick on the following weekend where forty-eight hours in Kenneth's company proved to be a real eye-opener. When joining Doncaster Bloodstock Sales in April of that year, I quickly discovered that Kenneth had only two gears - fast asleep or flat out - and his zest for life is perhaps his most outstanding quality.

His energy and enthusiasm -whether at work or play- are legendary and his ability to combine one with the other so successfully has undoubtedly increased his huge circle of friends from so many different walks of life.

An outstanding sportsman and a tough competitor who enjoys life to the full, Kenneth is a person who can be accurately described as unique. He has a legion of friends who all have an amazing tale to tell about their association with "Uncle Kenny" and you can be sure that the occasion in question gave him as much pleasure as the person concerned.

From Jack Berry
Racehorse Trainer, Lancashire.
I am honoured to have been asked to write a few words for Ken Oliver's book.

Ken, also known as the Benign Bishop, has worked and played hard all his life. He loves a bit of fun, is never known to jib at a drink, and on account of it he has been seen, on occasion, at dinner a bit worse for wear. One should never be fooled by him when seen in this well-oiled condition as any deals made would have been honoured. Next day he would have remembered every word said.

He is a great character and a gentleman to boot.

From Padge Berry
Bloodstock Agent, Wexford.
I left College at eighteen, bought my first horse a few months later and named him Johnnie Walker. We won a couple of point-to-points the following year and then I sent him to Goffs Sales, Ballsbridge. He was bought by one J.K.M. Oliver - a complete stranger - that same stranger is today my very best friend.

I found him an extraordinary man of many parts, a great man to hounds, a leading Amateur Rider, a top class Trainer of National Hunt Horses, the brain-child behind the revival of Doncaster Bloodstock Sales and numerous other activities. Ken's unlimited energy, combined with an astute brain and an ambition to be the best, made success that much easier. On the lighter side, the mischievous smile, the twinkle in the eyes and the love of a good party (asleep or awake) has endeared him to many.

To quote Rudyard Kipling "He filled the unforgiving minute with sixty seconds worth of distance run" giving a lot of friends lots of fun.

From T.D.C. Dun
Chairman of The Directors Royal Highland and Agricultural Society of Scotland.
My friend Kenneth - what a man! Auctioneer, estate agent, farmer, house builder, originator of Doncaster Bloodstock Sales and racehorse trainer - each one in it's own right a full time occupation for any normal mortal.

He still finds time to be Director of the Royal Highland Agricultural Society, Secretary of the Teviotdale Farmers' Club - Scotland's oldest, and before most of us are out of bed, to tend his immaculate garden.

His truly versatile sporting career, sadly interrupted by military service during the 1939-45 war, embraced his hobbies of rugby, tennis, squash, hunting and golf, the latter two of which he still enjoys.

However his finest sporting moments came in his days as a leading amateur National Hunt Jockey. "Win or lose, we'll have the booze". Kenneth's favourite quote says it all.

A great companion - he enjoys a full and interesting life. Doubtless you will enjoy a full and interesting book.

Josh Gifford
Racehorsetrainer, Sussex.
Ken Oliver what can be written or said that is not already to be told in this book.

A day at the Sales, an interesting gelding is led in and Ken starts the bidding with a few passing quips to the assembled audience. Now a few firm bids flow, then I make my play, the bidding goes on at great speed and wit, suddenly the hammer falls. Good God, I have a gelding, two grand more than I had intended to bid, such is the man.

Later in the year brings the exclusive "Honourable Group of Racing Golfers" together, for the "world famous" gathering at Muirfield. Firstly Ken has a word to the principals at the Club, the British Open Championship date must be changed next year, it coincides with his following year fixture - all will be taken care of! The competition itself, which is over two days, is won by the last person out, riding in a Buggie stashed up with vintage port, some might say an unfair advantage. The "before" dinner speech starts with the customary bedlam. This is soon stopped by the sheer presence of the great man. He commands complete respect and soon Ken decides that the dinner must proceed and gently slides back into his chair with well rehearsed precision to silently preside over us.

But back to horses, Ken rode the winner of the 1950 Scottish Grand National on his own Sanvina, and one of her direct descendants, Deep Sensation, won two great races for me at the Cheltenham National Hunt Festival and Aintree's Grand National Meeting in 1993. Ken was voted National Hunt Breeder for the 1992/93 season as a result.

A gentleman and friend to everyone, we enjoy his generosity and sincerity, we all love him dearly.

From Charles Smith,
Farmer and ex-amateur rider, Roxburghshire.
It is fitting that we pay tribute to Kenneth's wife Rhona.

Rhona Wilkinson of Whitehaugh, Hawick has been a horsewoman all her life - from the days when we all showed ponies together at Hawick Show. She will be remembered amongst other things, for her great horse, Wyndburgh.

In 1958 Kenneth entered the greatest partnership of his life when they got married. At that time Kenneth held a permit to train and from that foundation Rhona and he went forward to found their well-known Scottish Racing Stable at Hassendean Bank. Rhona has the unique ability to attend to the actual training of the horses as well as all the bookwork associated with a stable. Of course, she also has the often taken for granted job of seeing to all the domestic details which make life pleasant.

Rhona and Kenneth have been well coupled and each respects and admires the other. Kenneth has achieved much, thanks to the loving help and support of his wife.

1

THE BORDER OLIVERS

The Scottish Borders is a land apart lying as its name suggests between England and Scotland. It is a territory rich in history and, even now, centuries after the days of the reivers and their raids across the Tweed to capture the cattle, sheep and even the women of their neighbours, the traditions live on in the annual common ridings and festivals of towns such as Hawick, Jedburgh and Kelso which regularly provide a disproportionate representation in Scotland's rugby team. The Borderer is something different and someone liable to defy any attempt at mere classification.

In truth this is a land where sport in all its senses courses through the blood of the natives. Of all the activities close to the heart of the Borderer none transcends the horse. After all it was a sturdy and rugged horse which carried such characters as Wat o' Harden and Johnnie Armstrong into England to replenish their larders. Today the Borders is a land of peace, but nowhere else in the United Kingdom can one ride the hills or follow the hounds with such freedom or enjoy such sport. This is the land of the Bold Buccleuch, the Jedforest, the Lauderdale, the Berwickshire, the Liddesdale, the College Valley and the Border. Anyone from the shires who follows a Border pack soon comes to terms with foxhunting as it should be, and to follow a huntsman over the rolling hills requires both skill and a mount equal to the task.

Inevitably the Border hunts have over many years produced an outstanding succession of point-to-pointers, hunter chasers and top class steeplechasers. The annals of National Hunt racing ring loud with such names as The Callant, Earl's Brig, Flying Ace, Freddie, Rubstic, The Benign Bishop and, of course, that unluckiest of all who have faced the Aintree challenge - Wyndburgh. To that list one can add such names as

11

Merryman, Spud Tamson, Dun Boy, Bright Beach and many more. The men and women who have produced these horses are equally renowned - Charlie Scott, Jimmy Scott Aiton, Reg and Betty Tweedie, Billy Hamilton, the Dun family - Robin, Tommy, Geordie, Michael and Peter - and of course as this story will tell - Ken and Rhona Oliver.

Oliver is very much a Border name and none have made it ring louder throughout the land than Kenneth Oliver. Now, as he approaches eighty years of age, Ken can look back on a life so full of achievements, thrills and sheer unrivalled fun that it never ceases to amaze all those who have had the chance to cross his path. For sure, to have known Ken Oliver in any guise is something that no-one is ever likely to forget. This then is the tale of a man who since Stewart Wight retired, has been Scotland's most successful trainer, a brilliant amateur jockey, an excellent golfer, a distinctly useful tennis player, livestock and bloodstock auctioneer, hard-headed businessman, farmer, gardener, husband and father and friend and confidante to many. To say it has been a full life is but the wildest of understatements.

There is no better example, if one has to be found, of Ken's almost eternal lust for life than when just two years ago after he had attended the funeral of the Kelso farmer and master cattle breeder Tom Brewis, he said to the woman minister, Marion Dodd: "My dear, that was a wonderful service you conducted for poor Tom. I would very much like to book you for mine - but mind you, it will not be for many years yet!"

Marion Dodd, was one of many links in the chain of Ken's varied life in that her father, Harry Dodd, was also a well-known minister in the Church of Scotland in several Border parishes. He eventually retired to the village of Denholm, near Hawick, and over the years played many a round of golf with Ken at the local course at Minto. In turn, Harry Dodd's brother Percy was one of those characters that life throws up every so often, although perhaps less so nowadays than fifty years ago. Percy Dodd was larger than life as Ken fondly remembers: "Percy did everything with an extraordinary zest. He farmed at Old Greenlaw, but his first love was racing and he trained for a number of years. We used to see quite a bit of each other and played tennis in the Scottish Championships in the late 1940's at Peebles. We were up against a pair of pretty dour and pompous Germans and with Percy and I having had a couple of gins beforehand we were in a bright mood. Well, the Germans couldn't take our fun and just packed up and left."

Ken rode various winners for Percy Dodd, including several at that now sadly defunct course at Rothbury in North Northumberland. It was a place where fun abounded: "I remember an occasion when I rode one of my own horses - Stockwhip - to win at Rothbury. That was grand but I forgot that I was also due to act as auctioneer for the selling race later in the card. Suddenly there was a call for me to go to the weighing room to conduct the sale." And from that point things definitely started to go wrong with a vengeance. "Usually at Rothbury they brought a chair into the unsaddling enclosure for the auctioneer to stand on, but on this occasion a friend of mine, Ernie Johnston, had been up to mischief and had sawed one of the legs almost through. When I stood up on the chair the whole thing collapsed in a heap with me sprawling on the ground. Behind me was Captain Scott Briggs, the senior steward, and he was heard to remark something less than complimentary about the demeanour of his officials." Obviously officialdom was not amused.

Incidents such as those have been part of Ken Oliver's life almost since he was old enough to walk. It has been a life packed to the full, but above all else one involving people and friendships. So where did it all begin? Well, as in any form of livestock breeding the roots have to be found in the pedigree and on the land and countryside where he was raised. Ken's father, Douglas Oliver, was the most wonderful gentleman in the true sense of the word. I (Dan Buglass) have personal memories of him in his declining years and for all his great age - he was one of the last to have memories of fighting the Boers in South Africa - and the sense of awe in which he was held by the local farming community as the managing director of Andrew Oliver and Son Ltd, livestock auctioneers in Hawick, he was never too busy to stop and chat with anyone. Ken was lucky enough to inherit much of that charm and wisdom, and well he has used it through the years.

The maternal side of the pedigree similarly sprang from a tried and proven line. Sybil Brown came from a well-known manufacturing family in the Galashiels area and while she had no great sporting ambitions, she produced a family of three daughters and a son who, each in their own way, excelled in life. Memory can play tricks all too easily, but Ken has no doubt that he was born lucky and had the most marvellous parents who gave their love and interest throughout their long lives. His childhood was truly wonderful.

James Kenneth Murray Oliver was born on February 1st, 1914, just as the clouds of war were gathering over Europe. Happily, the young Oliver children were well insulated from the chaos and carnage which ensued. It was, however, a sad time for the local farming community as the war memorials of the area testify. Home was Hasseddean Bank, a 400-acre holding on the estate of the Earl of Minto, five miles east of the town of Hawick with its busy textile mills. It was, and still is, in an idyllic situation with the farmhouse looking due south towards the River Teviot and the village of Denholm and the Cheviot Hills. Real hunting country.

Ken had three older sisters - Florence, Muriel and Elsie. Because he was the baby of the family he was bullied and teased, but really it was all good fun and they were very close. In their day Muriel and Elsie proved to be no mean sports and both of them represented Scotland at hockey on several occasions. The surrounding countryside was a playground for any youngster and the Oliver children went on frequent long walks with their mother as Ken remembers: "We often used to go through the Nutbank Wood and then on past Minto House and up on to the Crags where mother, having obtained the key from the estate factor, we used to have picnics at Fatlips Castle. They were great days."

To this day Fatlips Castle stands high on the Crags overlooking the Teviot giving a commanding panorama to the east and then to the south and the English border from where in former times the bold men of Northumberland would dash to repay Scottish misdeeds - a veritable playground for the young and bold Oliver!

It was also on these walks that Ken developed a passion for nature and flowers which still endures: "We used to pick primroses and cowslips on those picnic trips with mother and I suppose from then on I just loved to have flowers and more than that to grow them." Green fingers were in evidence from then on and at the age of eight he was prepared to let the world see what he could do: "I decided that I would stage an exhibition of my flowers at the local Minto Flower Show. I think some people were a bit surprised at what I had done." Nowadays, no-one visits Ken at Hassedean Bank without a walk through the gardens and greenhouses - all four of them!

The social life of the Borders has always been a busy one and Ken and his sisters were keen attenders at the round of childrens' parties. One of those occasions in particular sticks in his memory: "It was at one of the grander houses near Hawick where I saw this rather podgy boy standing in a corner all on his own crying his eyes out, so I went over to try and cheer him up. I didn't manage to make him stop, but we became friends." That little podge turned out to be none other than the young Willie Whitelaw (now Lord Whitelaw, the famous politician) and that chance encounter forged a true friendship: "I never imagined that he would one day become such an outstanding and respected politician and statesman. We are still friends to this day and meet racing and on the golf course at Muirfield."

Ken's first introduction to the equestrian scene was not without its difficulties, and indeed it very nearly put him off for life. "Father used to hunt and was very keen that I should ride so he bought me a pony. He was a Shetland and a bit of a brute to put it mildly. One day I was trying to get him through a small gate in front of the house and into a big field. He just would not budge, but just then the shepherd came along and gave him one almighty whack on the backside. We were off - right out into the middle of the field where he then proceeded to stop dead in his tracks with the inevitable result that I flew straight over his head and landed on the ground with a great thump." The reaction was predictable: "I have had enough of this carry-on. No more for me!" Happily for Ken and the racing world this initial fall was soon forgotten. There would be many more.

Education is a necessity in life and Douglas Oliver determined that his young son should have the best. First, at the age of seven he was sent off to board at Warriston Preparatory School in Moffat, Dumfriesshire. Being packed off to school, particularly if one is leaving behind a happy home is not the most pleasant of experiences, and it was no different back in 1921 for the young Ken: "I think I must have cried all the way there and for a few days after that, but once I settled in I enjoyed the life there."

From Warriston the next move was to one of Scotland's best known public schools - Merchiston Castle in Edinburgh. Merchiston has a long and honourable tradition of educating prominent Scots, many of whom have gone on to make their mark in the world. Bankers, Cabinet Ministers and eminent surgeons have all come from that establishment but it has also always been a school famed for its sporting prowess. Countless fine golfers, but especially rugby players, have been Merchistonians - and many of them with farming blood in their veins. Such an environment was tailor-made for the young Ken.

Those days at Merchiston are still fondly remembered: "I really enjoyed myself there. I made many friends during my time, and many of them remain close friends to this day. One good friend was Ian Robertson, and he's done not too badly ending up as a senior Scottish Judge, Lord Robertson."

Sport was Ken's passion at Merchiston: "I was lucky to be good enough to play rugby for the First XV and cricket for the First XI and took part in just about every type of game I could find time for." However, the academic field was less fervently pursued: "I was bottom of every class I could possibly be, with the exception of mathematics." That latter success will surprise no-one, for throughout his business career the acumen of Ken Oliver has been a force to be reckoned with and a deal struck was a deal to be kept by all parties. School discipline, not unnaturally, was not always to his liking: "I must have broken each and every rule and regulation that I could, but they were great days and I got on well with the masters - I think they knew that I was never one who would conform."

Towards the end of his school days Ken began to think seriously about a career. It was a time that brought a degree of tension and anxiety. "I wasn't at all sure that I wanted to join my father in the family business as an auctioneer, but after a while I made up my mind that I did not want to disappoint him so I resolved that that's what I would do."

It was a decision that Ken has never regretted. "I joined him in 1932, and after a few months I knew this was the life for me - I really began to enjoy myself and to understand what my father, uncle and grandfather had done in establishing the name of Andrew Oliver and Son in the farming world. I wanted to be a part of all that."

2

THE FAMILY BUSINESS

The early 1930's were not happy times in the farming industry and even to this day there are men and women all over the United Kingdom who recall with more than a degree of bitterness those bleak years which brought many to their knees and not a few to bankruptcy. The seeds of the depression, from which in truth the whole country suffered, were sown in the euphoria which followed the end of the First World War. The returning troops were promised a "Land Fit for Heroes." They were to be sorely disappointed and gravely disillusioned.

For farmers it was not easy to make the adjustment from the high prices of war, when the Government would buy everything they could produce regardless of the cost. From 1920 onwards farming passed through depression to a total slump which was only relieved in the late 1930's by the prospect of yet another conflict. Prices of both crops and livestock fell back disastrously, and indeed it is on record that lambs sold off the Border hills in 1931 were making exactly the same values as they had during the Napoleonic wars - all of 120 years before. This then is the business environment into which the young and enthusiastic Ken Oliver started his career as an auctioneer with the family firm of Andrew Oliver and Son Ltd. It was to be a path which led in many diverse and interesting directions.

But before we progress further it is time to look back and consider the founding of Andrew Oliver and Son Ltd, livestock auctioneers. The story truly begins with an entry in the records of Eckford Parish Church, near Kelso: "James Oliver, tenant of Marlefield Hope. His child was born on 20th September, 1793, and baptised on 22nd October, 1793 ... named Andrew." The minister who penned those words could little have imagined that he had just recorded the first details of the life of the man who was to found the oldest livestock mart in the United Kingdom. Andrew Oliver was obviously a man of great vision and what he saw in the way of the marketing of agricultural produce clearly did not satisfy his ideas of fair play. Indeed the old trysts and fairs where cattle and sheep were brought by dealers after having been purchased from farmers and then sold on to farmers in the south for fattening had changed little for hundreds of years.

Andrew Oliver served his apprenticeship as a solicitor in Kelso before setting up on his own account in Annan, near Dumfries. After a brief spell he moved to Hawick in 1817 and set up in business as a Writer and Auctioneer - writer being the old Scottish term for lawyer. Andrew Oliver was not a man slow to trumpet his own capabilities. His business card read thus: "Andrew Oliver, Messenger, Auctioneer, etc, begs leave to announce to his friends and public in general, that he has commenced business in Hawick, and from his prompt attention to business, and the great practice he already has had, hopes to merit a share of public favour. He flatters himself that those who may honour him with their employment in any of these branches will meet with satisfaction."

He continued in the same vein, saying, "Andrew Oliver executes respectable sales as an auctioneer and likewise as an appraiser. N.B. Andrew Oliver will attend at Newcastleton once a month."

The language is forthright and one can well imagine the need for a "respectable auctioneer" for history is not lacking in tales of farmers being swindled by silver-tongued dealers! The parallel with his descendant Kenneth is also clear, for 150 years later he saw the need for a similar code in the establishment of Doncaster Bloodstock Sales Limited.

Organising those early sales was no easy matter. Advertising was in its infancy and postage was very expensive - a letter from Hawick to London cost around 6p, which was a colossal sum in those days of the 1820's. Worse still was the formidable levels of taxation levied by the Government of the time - 7.5p on every advertisement in the newspapers. However, worst of all was the tax of 5% on the sale of all movables with a 3% tax on heritable property.

For auctioneers life was difficult, if not impossible, in that they had to give the Excise Authorities three clear days notice before a sale could be held and to present a full catalogue of all the goods to be sold. It seems that the rules and regulations of taxation in those days were not all that different from today and the machinations of the Customs and Excise over VAT.

18

In common with their counterparts today, the farmers of those times were not at all keen on taxation, so they managed to avoid the 5% tax by holding informal sales out in the country. However, these were far from satisfactory and the young Andrew Oliver found his business steadily growing. The breakthrough came in 1846 when Sir Robert Peel repealed the protectionist Corn Laws and at the same time the tax on auctions. This was Andrew Oliver's moment, and he grabbed it, although progress at first was slow.

He started a series of monthly sales in Hawick in Slitrig Crescent and this site can be said to have been the first auction mart in Britain. The sales were not large at first as the records for 1851 show:-

```
1 Kyloe cow   £3  17  6
1  "    "    "  £4   0  0
1 Grey Mare   £7  15  0
Total         £15  12  6
```

The total for the twelve sales held in that year was a modest £535, but it was a beginning, although Andrew Oliver is said to have come very close to giving up and concentrating on his legal business which was much more renumerative. He died in 1857 and was succeeded by his son James Oliver. This Oliver proved to be a real man of action.

In 1860 James acquired new premises in Bourtree Place in Hawick and in the same year advertised his first sale of store lambs when only around 200 were sold. This was the foundation of the huge sales which were later to be held in Hawick of both sheep and cattle from the surrounding areas. The advent of the railway to Hawick was another great boon and soon farmers from all over the United Kingdom were seeking stock bred on the high Border hills. The sheep and the cattle were, as auctioneers say, "good doers." In other words healthy and of sound constitution.

The numbers passing through the mart increased rapidly, first passing 20,000 and then 50,000, so that before long a new site had to be found to cope with the business. After a century of selling in its mart, and another move to still larger premises in Hawick, Andrew Oliver and Son were selling well over 200,000 sheep plus large numbers of cattle. The largest recorded sale was on August 22nd, 1884, when 28,155 sheep passed through the ring; while over three days in August, 1907 no less than 60,450 were sold.

James Oliver was joined in business by his son Andrew in 1875 and still later his younger son Douglas - the father of Kenneth - entered the firm.

As auctioneers the Olivers obviously had many close connections with farmers and in due course became farmers themselves. James Oliver became tenant of the farm of Flex, just outside Hawick, in 1810 while his son Andrew was tenant of both Borthwickmains and Howcleugh. Similarly Douglas Oliver acquired the tenancy of Hassendean Bank in 1901 on his return from the Boer War. James Oliver died in 1905 at the grand old age of eighty-eight, and was by all accounts active almost to the very last days of his long and busy life.

As any farmer knows full well, values of livestock can and do change over the years - and not always in a favourable direction. Throughout his life Andrew Oliver kept a full and comprehensive diary and it is interesting to note his observations on this topic. Writing in 1891, he noted: "I have seen many changes and great fluctuations in prices, and it is interesting to recall them for it may happen again. In 1882 I sold the Half-bred draft ewes from the farm of Hallrule for 70/- and this past year at 36/3. Cheviot ewes from Sundhope in 1882 made 44/- while this year they sold for 15/-." Perhaps then there is a lesson for all breeders of livestock, including producers of bloodstock - prices do not rise forever without a blip in the market. It's staying power that matters.

Close friendships are often made through business dealings and that certainly proved to be the case with the Olivers. The friendships have lasted over the generations so that today Ken Oliver can trace his family links with such names as the Elliots of Hindhope, near Jedburgh, back well over 100 years. Indeed the Elliots of Hindhope were among the first to realise that selling their pedigree Cheviot rams through a mart such as Hawick was a much better way of doing business than haggling with a neighbour over a stone wall over the price of a ram. Ram sales were from the start highly popular and even as early as 1861 almost 300 were sold on one single day. Here again Andrew Oliver recorded the prices of many of those rams: "The highest I got was £120 for Lord Herries which was sold by Mr. Elliot of Hindhope, though my father did get £194 5s for one from Mr. Brydon of Kinnelhead, Beattock."

By 1945 those sales of rams had grown enormously to over 1,000 head, so that the sale had to be divided into two days with customers coming from far and near as well as a notable export trade to such destinations as Norway, New Zealand, Australia, the Falkland Islands, South Africa, Canada and several South American destinations.

In the early days most of the stock was walked or driven to Hawick and transported out by rail, unless sold locally, so it is fair to say that the auction mart brought considerable business to the town of Hawick and market days were certainly occasions when the shopkeepers expected their tills to ring loudly. However, moving stock by rail was never entirely successful - delays would occur and it could be some considerable time before a buyer might get his purchases delivered home, and then they might not always arrive in the best condition. And so road transport developed. It was a slow progress after the First World War, but by 1931 over 30,000 sheep were being moved out of the mart on lorries and thereafter the trend continued until first the railways stopped transporting any livestock and then finally closed altogether through the Borders.

Andrew Oliver remained a bachelor throughout his life but he was a man who loved to travel and it is amazing to discover how he managed to visit such places as the South of France and Egypt in those days long before the package tour. From his diaries one can see that he also appreciated the finer things in life, not least of which appear to have been fine wines and good food. Obviously his nephew inherited some of those qualities.

But if Andrew Oliver had a passion in life apart from business it has to have been hunting and racing. He followed both sports with marvellous resolution and his hunting diary makes fascinating reading. The first entry is for Saturday 9th November, 1872:- "Hunting for the first time in my life. The Duke's (of Buccleuch) met and I rode to the meet with Mr Edward Wilson. My mount was a well-bred chestnut gelding called Charley. We had a good day's sport."

He was obviously smitten from the start and thereafter hunted as often as his business commitments would allow. The hunting field was then, as it is today, a place for sport and meeting people and here Andrew Oliver certainly broadened his circle. The diary note for 10th January, 1888, makes that clear:- "Met at Groundistone with the Duke's and had a great run. The company was very large, upwards of 70 riders including, His Grace the Duke of Buccleuch, Lord Dalkeith, Lord George Scott, Lord Henry Scott, Lord Herbett Scott, Sir George Douglas, Mr C.J. Cunningham, Major Lockhart and several ladies."

Andrew Oliver became a shrewd judge of a horse and over the years had many outstanding hunters of which one of his favourites was undoubtedly Howcleugh. Repeatedly he mentions how well Howcleugh performed though he did have the occasional fall as he recorded on 1st December 1900: "Hunting on Howcleugh. Met at Drinkstone but poor sport. My horse fell with me above Calaburn and I got a nasty tumble and bruised my ribs rather badly!" Such incidents, however, did not dampen his enthusiasm for the chase.

Racing was another passion with Andrew Oliver as he remarked in his diary: "Racing is one of the sports I have enjoyed as much as any other, and though I have done a little myself and won a few races, it has been more as an onlooker at meetings that I have taken part in the game. I have always admired a good horse, especially a thoroughbred, and I think there is nothing finer than seeing a well contested race, where blood, condition and good jockeyship are fighting for the mastership." His nephew Kenneth has always been of the same opinion.

It is quite incredible to realise how many meetings Andrew Oliver attended over the years in the days before the motor car. He travelled to Musselburgh, Ayr, Hamilton, Bogside, Annan, Oatridge, Dunbar, Rothbury, Hexham, York, Newcastle, Carlisle, Manchester, Liverpool, Ascot and Doncaster. Many of these courses are of course mere mentions in the history books now, but he does say that Ascot and Doncaster were his "favourites".

He managed to see most of the top races, both over fences and on the flat and was at Epsom in 1888 when Ayrshire won the Derby and Seabreeze the Oaks. He even raced in Ireland at Leopardstown and Phoenix Park, but the race he clearly loved above all was the Grand National. He saw Gamecock win in 1887, Playfair in 1888, Ilex in 1890 and right on without missing a year through to Jenkinstown's win in 1910. The National was then, and still is today, a great social occasion and Andrew Oliver seldom travelled to Liverpool alone. Indeed it seems as though half the farmers in the Hawick area made the trip each year. He says of those times: "I often recall happy meetings in the smoke room of the Exchange Station Hotel or at the American bar." That love of Liverpool still runs in the Oliver family today. The St. Leger meeting at Doncaster was another "must" on his calendar and he was there to see Seabreeze follow up her triumph in the Oaks by taking the oldest of all the Classics. He also witnessed the great Persimmon's win at Doncaster in 1896. Andrew Oliver and his nephew, Kenneth, had much in common and in an amazing quirk of fate he mentions the sales at Doncaster: "The town is celebrated for its yearling sales of bloodstock, and in their large paddocks on the four race days Messrs. Tattersall dispose of drafts from the most distinguished breeders. I have often attended them, and it is a most interesting sight and well worth a visit." Little did Andrew know that his nephew would be instrumental in resurrecting those sales after they fell into decline.

Royal Ascot was another firm favourite and between 1894 and 1911 he never missed a year. The three races which clearly held his attention most were The Stakes, The Hunt Cup and The Gold Cup. The winners of these races were faithfully recorded in his diary, including of course Persimmon's win in The Gold Cup in 1897. The Manchester November Handicap was another favourite race: "I have often been present and always enjoyed it, though the weather has been wet and cold, and the colours of the riders and the horses themselves hardly distinguishable by the fog, which has caused racing to be abandoned some days altogether." Manchester was ever thus!

Like his nephew fifty years later, Andrew Oliver was a keen amateur rider and won several races. The first was the Challenge Cup for the Border Mounted Rifles at Kelso in June 1876 which he won by a head on Hero in a field of seven. In later years, however, he chose to put a younger pilot up and a certain Tom Douglas appears to have been the favoured jockey, though it was Mr J. M. Bell who won the Buccleuch Cup at Kelso on Howlcleugh for him in April 1899, after having been prepared for the race by the Dunbar trainer, John McCall. Fifty years later in 1949 Andrew Oliver's nephew - one Mr. J.K.M. Oliver was to win precisely the same race on his own horse, Johnnie Walker.

Andrew Oliver was a truly amazing man, who despite a zest for sport including shooting, coursing and curling in addition to hunting and racing, never neglected the family business which by this time was expanding rapidly. However, in later years his younger brother Douglas gradually assumed a larger share of responsibilities. This then was the heritage to which the young Kenneth Oliver was born and to which he was to devote the next fifty years of his life.

3

PRE-WAR POINT-TO -POINT WINNERS

To master any profession it is essential that a new entrant should start at the bottom, and this is particularly true for the aspiring auctioneer. It has certainly never been a case of jumping up into the rostrum and selling virtually anything from the very first day. And so it was that the young Kenneth Oliver began working with the family firm in 1932 very much as the office junior. He worked his way from the bottom upwards - though not unsurprisingly he climbed the ladder with some alacrity.

Ken soon warmed to his chosen career and began to master the secrets of the auction business and the little bits and pieces of information that are part and parcel of the trade as well as noting the informed gossip. Times were hard for farmers then and there was, as indeed there still is today, a feeling that those who purchased from farmers prospered rather more than the primary producer. Ken remembers one such incident in Hawick: "There was great antagonism against butchers, both on the part of the farmers and from the townspeople who thought that they were being charged far too much for meat. However, Dod Ormiston, who was a local meat trader, decided that he would start selling both mutton and beef from a stall in the Common Haugh in Hawick. It caused a fearful row and while his meat was much cheaper it didn't last for long. Everyone has to make a living and farmers need butchers just as much as the butchers need the farmers."

Many of the local butchers were customers in the mart where they bought their weekly supplies and of course these transactions had to be carefully recorded in the ledgers by the clerks. A job for young Oliver, but before being let loose the head cashier, John Hogg, thought he had better check the young man's capabilities: "Mr. Kenneth. I would like to test

25

your handwriting."

"That will be fine, Mr. Hogg, I will get a pen, but what would you like me to write or copy?"

The command was somewhat unexpected: "Write down one hundred times - where there is drink there is danger!"

The task was duly accomplished, but the message was not entirely taken on board and all throughout his life Ken has enjoyed a civilised drink and a good party. "And why not?" he asks, "Life is for living, and I've done many a deal over a drink, and it certainly has never affected my memory." Indeed, and there is many an individual who can testify to Ken telephoning the next morning after a mighty night just to remind that person of the business conducted the previous evening. Someone years ago remarking at his amazing capacity said: "That bloody man Oliver has a memory like an elephant. He never forgets no matter how big a party he's had!"

Ken's first undertaking as a "real auctioneer" was to sell the pigs - a traditional starting point for the "boy" in the team. "I didn't get on too badly, my father had of course coached me and having watched what was happening in the mart during my school holidays I had a pretty fair idea of how things should go." However, that first sale did not go entirely to plan: "There was some sort of a mix-up and one pig was wrongly delivered so the next day I had to sort things out. I put this young pig in a bag on my back and set off on the motorcycle my father had given me."

The journey was somewhat eventful: "I was heading for the Arks Farm, right out on the Carter Bar, which was quite a trip. I had barely started out when the pig piddled and for the next twenty miles that damned pig pissed down my neck and back. I never knew that a little pig could pee so much."

However, all work and no play was not to be the régime and as Ken began work as auctioneer he was on the verge of one of the major steps in his life. He remembers it well: "I suppose apart from my mother and father few other people have had as great an influence on me as Tommy and Jean Elliot who farmed just outside Hawick at Burnfoot and also in the Cheviot Hills at Attonburn. They were so kind to me and Tommy helped me enormously by encouraging me and introducing me to very many farmers. That helped me greatly because as an auctioneer you have to know people and remember their names."

But there was more: "I hadn't ridden since the episode with the Shetland pony and in fact I wasn't all that interested because I was playing rugby for Hawick "A". Tommy went to my father and said - Douglas, we've got to get Kenneth on hunting." From then on there was no stopping him. "I would wait by the telephone on a Friday night for Tommy to ring and ask me if I would like to hunt Jean's mare Mattie. I never refused."

The Duke of Buccleuch's Hunt is without doubt Scotland's premier pack. Its country is immense, stretching from the Dumfries border and covering all of Roxburghshire on the north side of the Teviot and all of Selkirkshire. It's a very varied country with miles and miles of grassy hills and then arable land further down. To hunt with the Buccleuch needs a good horse and a firm nerve. Some years ago when Michael Clayton, editor of *Horse and Hound* hunted with the Buccleuch and the then huntsman, Lionel Salter, he wrote: "Stone walls, five-bar gates and deep ditches are nothing to the Buccleuch. They take them all in their stride."

The Buccleuch have had some marvellous huntsmen over the years including one of the current masters, Trevor Adams, as well as Tom Smith and of course Lionel Salter. But above all of them the name of George Summers reigns supreme. He was quite exceptional and one can see in the fine portrait of him which hangs in the Duke of Buccleuch's home at Bowhill, near Selkirk, something special in the eyes and demeanour of the man. It was said by those who followed him that Summers could produce a good day's hunting even without a scent and that he could conveniently arrange for the hounds to run straight back to the kennels towards the end of a hard day. His help and advice did much to kindle Ken's lust for the chase: "He was a simply marvellous man and I doubt if there has ever been anyone like him who knew so much about hounds and hunting. A true genius."

Another to set Ken on course for later heroics was George Hedley. George farmed extensively in the Borders and was one of the most affable characters of his age. Easily recognisable with his check tweeds and sideburns he was typical of so many Border farmers in having an eye for a good horse and a love of seeing his colours in action at the local point-to-point meetings. George and Ken were firm friends and had many happy hours together.

George had a young horse named Delman of whom he had high hopes, especially since he was a full brother to one of the fastest horses in the country, Dochan-Doris. Delman was in fact the only horse ever to run in George Hedley's colours, but his father - also George - was a keen racing man with horses in training at Middleham in Yorkshire. This fact never ceased to amaze Ken: "George Hedley senior was notoriously careful with his money and once demonstrated that by giving a winning jockey a sack of potatoes as a present." On another occasion he and his wife were driving to Ayr when Mrs. Hedley asked him to stop so that she could visit the toilet. For that purpose she had to ask her husband for the necessary penny, to which he enquired: "Are you sure it's not just wind, my dear?".

In any event Ken and the younger George were frequent companions on the hunting field and in due course it was suggested that Ken might like to make his début on Delman.

Ken takes up the tale: "Before we finally decided to run Delman there was a trial of several point-to-pointers on the gallops at Midshiels, just up the road from Hassendean Bank where Harry Bell was later to make a name for himself in every sense of the word as a National Hunt trainer. Well, George and his father gave me a leg up on Delman and then we were off. But the bugger hung like hell and very nearly put me in a wood. I came back feeling pretty foolish and imagined that this would be the end of me riding the following Saturday."

However, father and son Hedley, had more faith: "You'll ride the horse on Saturday at the Lauderdale meeting", which in those days was held at Blainslie. But, it wasn't quite as simple as that, as Ken well remembers: "I had a very big decision to make, because Hawick Rugby Club - the famous Greens - were very short of players for the Saturday and I had been invited to play for the First XV as a centre three quarter for the very first time. You don't turn down an invitation to play for Hawick lightly. I made the choice to ride and of course I was never ever considered again for Hawick."

Blainslie was one of the most testing of all courses between the flags with a steep rise right to the top of the hill where both horse and rider could take a breather, then a fairly hair-raising downhill run before swinging back into the home straight. Blainslie was a true test for any horse and it took a steady nerve to tackle the fences which were always formidable. It was also a marvellous course for spectators, but by the same token it could be the coldest place on earth when the wind was in the east or north, and it was a most unwise racegoer who failed to pack something spiritual for warmth.

It was an anxious time for the young Oliver but as he waited for his race in the spring of 1935 he had the privilege of watching one of the all-time heroes of the Northern scene, Jimmy Patterson of Terrona, near Langholm, win his very last race on the great horse, Jaunty. Delman's race had a field of nineteen and the race is still etched firmly in the memory of the jockey: "Delman was a bit of a character and worse still he only had one eye. Well, I tell you this - we went into the first two fences with only one eye between the pair of us. Mine were tight shut, but he gave me a good feel and my confidence increased. This is great I thought, and heavens above he just kept improving and we won quite handily."

Not many riders are lucky enough to win on their first outing, and as Ken recounts: "You know what happened thereafter - we had a bit of a celebration!"

Yes, that was the first of very many parties that followed an Oliver triumph. Ken's philosophy to the triumphs and disasters of racing were never better summarised than when five years ago at Newbury with his High Edge Grey well backed for the Hennessy Gold Cup he was interviewed live on television by Julian Wilson for *BBC Grandstand*. Julian posed the question: "Now Ken you're quite a man for a party, what will you do if your horse wins?" The answer was to the point: "Julian, win or lose, we'll have the party." In any event High Edge Grey slipped up at the fourteenth fence, but there was still one great party.

But back to 1935 and Delman. After Blainslie it was on to the Border Union at Cornhill-on-Tweed. That first success was not to be repeated: "We were baulked at a fence and I came off but I remounted and still managed to finish third." Next was the Dumfriesshire at Lockerbie and more misfortune: "We were heading downhill towards a dip where there had been a wire fence which they had taken down. However, some silly bugger had forgotten to fill the holes and we came tumbling down and the saddle split in two. I remembered nothing more until I came to and met a man who was to become a great friend - Dr. John Sinclair."

That good doctor was also a farmer in Caithness at the strangely named Nottingham Mains and in future years he was instrumental in forging a connection which resulted in large numbers of North Country Cheviot sheep being sold in Hawick at the mart. As ever Ken was on the look out for a business opportunity. But storm clouds were gathering with Ken's mother becoming particularly anxious over her son's thrills and spills and she eventually demanded of his father: "Douglas, you'll have to get Kenneth a decent horse before he breaks his neck."

And as he himself adds: "That fall was probably the best thing that could have happened to me because I then got two decent horses which did me well. One was a mare called Evadne which won quite a few races for me. The other was Don Juan and he won as well." It was not long before other owners recognised that young Oliver was a jockey who always gave his best and if a horse was in a position to win, then for sure there would be no lack of effort from Ken. The progression to riding under rules as amateur was inevitable and just before the Second World

War Ken was riding for several well-known trainers and owners, including Lord Joicey and Captain L. Scott Briggs whose horse MacMoffat came second in the Grand National in both 1939 and 1940.

The Borders has always been a breeding ground for top class hunters and chasers, largely on account of the stockmanship of the farming community. Only two miles down the road towards Jedburgh on the farm of Newton, the Robson Scott family for many years bred a string of grand horses, including a hunter mare that Ken was particularly taken with. However, it was not just the horses which marked out the Robson Scott stud, as Ken recalls: "When I bought that mare the head lad was Wat Notman, and what a family those Notmans have been over the years in the bloodstock industry." Pedigrees are important, and the Notmans have proved their line: "Wat's cousin was Danny, and in turn he was the father of Alec Notman, who until he retired recently worked so diligently for Sheik Mohammed at Dalham Hall, near Newmarket. In turn Wat's brother Bob was groom to my friend Alan Innes and Bob prepared several of Alan's horses for me to win on at point-to-points."

This love of hunting and racing was not entirely without a purpose, though which came first is difficult to say. In any event Ken saw that with the enormous interest in bloodstock in the Borders and Northumberland there was an opening for a specialist sale.

There had been a previous attempt by an Edinburgh firm of solicitors to establish the Caledonian Hunter Register whereby a list of horses for sale was kept, but as Ken says: "The thing never got going as they didn't really understand the business but I was quite convinced we could do it properly." As so often with a new venture Ken received enormous support and encouragement from his old friends and mentors, Tommy and Jean Elliot, who urged him to "have a go." The first sale was held in September 1937 and it certainly put the young auctioneer on his mettle: "My father had managed to persuade Walter, Duke of Buccleuch, to open the sales but I was in a bit of a fluster because we were getting behind time. The Duke made an excellent speech from the rostrum wishing us well and so on, but then it was my turn and oh dear, what a job I made of it when I opened my mouth. My first words were - now then, ladies and gentlemen, we've wasted enough time already, let's get on with the sale." Happily the duke saw the funny side of it all!

From the outset the Kelso Horse Sales proved to be a success with buyers coming from all over the country in search of sound bloodstock. One of the early commissions successfully executed by Captain Rupert de Warrene Rogers was to buy a mount for Winston Churchill and a photograph of the great man on that horse still hangs proudly at Hassendean Bank. In 1939 a delegation acting on behalf of the German Government were expected to attend, but the prospect of war put a stop to that.

The initial success of Kelso gave encouragement to farmers and breeders to produce hunters and potential National Hunt horses and in due course many of those made their mark throughout the country. That aspect is something which Ken still feels is worthy of encouragement today: "I have always thought that farmers in this part of the world with all their experience in rearing livestock would be ideally suited to bloodstock production. Also, with the EC so keen to cut back on agricultural production it would seem to be sensible to encourage something that is in demand. I have made various attempts to persuade the Government to help, and to be fair when Lord Sanderson of Bowden (another of Ken's host of distant relatives) was a Minister at the Scottish Office I did feel I was getting somewhere, but that now seems to have stalled. I just can't understand why the Government doesn't see the importance of the bloodstock industry to the economy. The French and the Irish certainly do."

After the war the Kelso Horse sales stepped up a gear with a spring sale instigated in April, 1947, with over 200 head forward. Later in an attempt to boost the reputation of Kelso further Ken staged one of his famous publicity stunts: "We had a hell of a party at the Buccleuch Arms in St. Boswells with people from all over the country." One particular character to make his mark at that notable party was Willie Stephenson - of whom more later. "Willie was like me - anything for fun. Well, we must have been making a bit of a noise, because in came the local policeman. Willie just walked up to him, smiled and then took off the bobby's hat, filled it with champagne and clapped it back on the poor man's head." Fortunately that policeman also had a sense of fun and joined the party with some relish.

Some of those visitors from the south actually arrived by light aircraft at Hassendeam Bank: "They landed on the haugh field which later became the gallops." In later years the sight of a plane landing at Hassendean Bank was almost commonplace as owners and other business contacts flew in either to buy cattle and sheep or to see their horses.

Many good horses were sold at the Kelso Sales over the years, some of which produced both a degree of humour and extra work for the senior auctioneer: "The trainer Wilfred Crawford - the most honest and straightforward of men - had this horse by Vulgan named Sir Daniel entered in the catalogue with a guarantee of soundness in wind, eye, heart and action. However, at the time of sale Wilfred produced a vet's certificate from Alec Tully which said that the horse missed one heartbeat in ten." Naturally enough Ken announced this from the rostrum - a fact later confirmed by the sales' senior steward, Alistair Paton. The horse was sold in the ring to Ted Greenaway who was a very keen racing man besides being the vet at Liverpool racecourse.

Ted Greenaway must have suffered some unexplained hearing difficulty that day because he soon announced that he would not take the horse. There followed a lengthy dispute which was only ended at the November meeting at Liverpool when Ken said: "Ted, I'm getting fed up with all this. I'll take the horse off you." Ken then sent the horse to Ireland and Padge Berry: "Things seemed to get even worse because Padge reckoned that it wasn't just the heart which was wrong but also his wind." The following spring Padge ran the horse in four point-to-points and won them all! Padge Berry was obviously impressed and decided to give the horse every chance by having him hobdayed to ease the wind problems. The result was a further five wins in point-to-points. From there he went on to win a bumper, or National Hunt flat race, at Baldoyle near Dublin, before being sold to Peter Cazalet, who was then at the peak of his training career, for 2,500 guineas.

Sir Daniel had a particular liking for Windsor and won several races there on the banks of the Thames. Ken takes up the story again: "Peter Cazalet took him to Cheltenham for the Festival meeting where under his jockey Mr. John Lawrence, later to become Lord John Oaksey and now well respected for his work in Channel 4 racing, he was winning in a canter. However, Lord Oaksey took the wrong course. Years later I told John the full story of Sir Daniel and he laughed his head off telling me we should have kept the horse in Scotland."

But stepping back in time briefly, in the late 1930's the storm clouds were once more gathering over Europe and Ken, like so many of his generation, knew that war was inevitable and that they would be in the thick of it as their fathers had been before them. When the time arrived he had no hesitation but it was still a sad time leaving his hunting and racing behind, but above all his father and mother and the business. It had taken less than ten years for Ken to become an established figure in the Borders both as an auctioneer and sportsman - not to say something of a character. No one knew what the future might hold, but he went off to war determined to make the best of it. As ever, he did.

Uncle Andrew on Howcleugh, winner of the Buccleuch Cup at Kelso in 1899. Ken won the same race exactly fifty years later.

c.1920. Muriel, Mother, Florence, Elsie and Ken.

1922. Ken and his father. The ponys name has long been forgotten.

1937. The Lauderdale Point-to-point at Blainslie. Ken is fifth, about to take off.

1938. The United Border Hunt point-to-point at Cornhill. Ken on Evadne at the last fence, before winning from Hugh Falconer on Jean Peel.

1940. Ken and Rufus Keogh hunt Army horses with the Buccleuch at Ashkirk.

1946. Hawick Show. Jean leads Susan on Fuzzy Peg. She had just won her class and was Champion Pony in the show.

1949. Ken winning the Buccleuch Cup at Kelso on Johnnie Walker.

4

1939 TO 1946

The early days of the Second World War were a time when few people apart from Winston Churchill and his immediate circle had little conception of the struggle which lay ahead. Indeed there was a body of opinion which saw little necessity for Great Britain to become involved in yet another European conflict. In their view it was an argument for the continentals and not one which should involve Britain. Memories of the awful carnage of 1914-18 were still too painful for many families.

The full reality of Hitler's intentions became clear as he first overwhelmed Poland and Czechoslovakia before turning his attentions to the Low Countries and France. It soon became obvious that this was to be a fight from which there was no question of turning aside. The very survival of Britain and its empire was at stake. Whether all the young men who joined up were fully aware of the enormity of the struggle ahead does not matter. They, including Ken and many of his friends and contemporaries, knew where their obligations lay. Among those friends - all of them farmers - were Alan Innes, Kay Robertson and Ted Connor. A bunch of likely lads if ever there was one, but true friends all of them. Ken has fond and enduring memories of those happy days: "Alan Innes farmed at Windywalls, near Kelso, and was a wonderful friend. We were at school at Merchiston together and thereafter went about almost everywhere in company and got up to at least our fair share of escapades as young men always will".

Alan Innes was also a man whose interests were very similar to Ken's; "He had an encyclopaedic knowledge of bloodstock and was very keen that we should have a really good horse between us. He also has a marvellous brain and one of the sharpest intellects I have ever come across.

Besides that he had a lovely sister called Joan in whom I had more than a passing interest!" In the fullness of time that interest was to lead to something rather more.

Kay Robertson came from another old Border family and farmed at Ladyrig, near Kelso. He sadly was to fall in action, but his memory lives on. "Kay was a great character and what a tragedy it was that he was killed at Anzio. He would have done so much with his life, and he was one who was forever looking to help others without thinking of himself." Tragedy, however, was no respecter of goodness. Kay's sister Betty carried on the family tradition in no uncertain terms and married Reg Tweedie. Together they trained the great Freddie and bred a whole succession of winners on the flat from their great mare Rosie Wings.

The cavalry remount school at Redford Barracks in Edinburgh with the Scots Greys was where this raw bunch of recruits were to spend the early days of the war and it certainly provided its share of experiences for Ken and his friends: "For the first six weeks we spent our time of the parade ground doing nothing else but bloody square bashing - which wasn't what we thought we had joined up for".

Subsequently events moved on apace: "After basic training we were told to go down to the riding school where we were split into two groups - those who had ridden before and those who hadn't. Not unnaturally we put ourselves down as having ridden before. Well, they put me on a grey cob which kicked, farted and bucked and generally messed about. At this an officious corporal appeared and said, get off that horse you know bugger all about riding, you've never been on a horse in all of your bloody rotten little life."

That appeared to be that for the time being, but the old connections soon came into play: "God, it was sheer hell being back on the square but I had an ally in Major Alvery Hall-Watt from Wooler in Northumberland. I met his batman in a pub and after a few drinks he realised that I had ridden a lot of point-to-point winners and the word got back that young Oliver was feeling pretty fed up." The consequences of that meeting were both rapid and highly satisfactory: "Within a few days I was in a gentleman's ride under the command of no less a person than Major Joe Dudgeon who had been captain of the British show-jumping team."

The major and the raw recruit soon became firm friends through their mutual love of all things equestrian: "He soon had me made up to lance corporal, though mind you it was as an acting unpaid lance corporal. And then we went off down to the Borders to hunt with the Buccleuch and my old pal Summer." The quality of the mounts which Major Joe provided for his young friend was indeed something special: "We had a most marvellous time and I tell you that one day's hunting sticks in my mind to this very day. I had never before ridden a horse quite like the one I was on that day. He was quite simply the best hunter I had ever sat on until then and I tell you Major Joe got a hold of all the best army horses then. We jumped absolutely everything - we just flew the lot. That horse was a complete revelation." Years later Ken met his old friend Major Joe again in Dublin: "He saw us standing at the ringside and came over to chat and after that we kept in close touch. He was a wonderful judge of a horse and the nicest of men."

But the days of hunting were not to last for long and soon it was on with the hard grind of soldiering, though during leave in 1941 Ken did find time to take that "interest" in Joan Innes to its logical conclusion by marrying her in Hawick. In due course that union was blessed with first a daughter Susan and after the war a son, Douglas Stuart.

From Redford Barracks Ken was sent south to an officers training course at Weedon cavalry school. There too the sporting links were soon forged with kindred spirits: "It was marvellous down there and I fell in with Gerald Balding, father of the successful trainers Ian and Toby, as well as being captain of the English polo team. I had the chance to ride some grand horses and I suppose the discipline must have done me some good." Also at Weedon was another man who became an abiding friend, Bryan Marshall - that wonderfully balanced jockey who was to win the Grand National on Early Mist in 1953 and Royal Tan the following year.

With basic training over it was on with the real war and into action. Commissioned into the Yorkshire Hussars Ken went first to the North African desert campaign and then it was over the Mediterranean to Sicily and subsequently the landings in southern Italy that were to pressage the ultimate victory.

Once in Italy it was not long before Ken found himself in hospital in Catania suffering from both malaria and jaundice. The Oliver sense of fun and lust for life soon surfaced: "Things were not good and for a while I was feeling pretty rough and the diet was plain. We were desperate for eggs and after a while we managed to persuade some of the local girls who cleaned the wards - at some considerable risk to themselves - to smuggle some in for us. And you know this - they used to bring them to us in their tits. They were very near hard-boiled before we got them!"

Lying in a hospital bed is not something that many people actively enjoy, and certainly not the recovering Oliver. His mind was as active and sharp as it has always been with the result that he wrote a letter to his father which was to have major ramifications in later life. "I said, dad, do you remember what you told me about the First World War at the time when Knight, Frank and Rutley were just getting off the ground? Well, when I get home after the war I think we should have a go." And have a go Oliver father and son certainly did.

Home after the war was Denholm House in the village of Denholm, just across the River Teviot from Hassendean Bank. It was a different world that Ken returned to with a wife and a young daughter and besides much had happened since 1939. Of those missing years he says: "I think I lost six years when I might have ridden quite a few winners." At first, the prospect of even sitting on a horse was a distant one: "I weighed in at thirteen stones in my birthday suit, and the army doctors told me that I would never be fit enough to ride again. Bugger them, I thought. I'll damned well show them." He did.

But first things first, and that meant getting back into harness in the business of Andrew Oliver and Son Ltd. His father was "not as young as he used to be, but still had a great grip of business." For the farming industry those years immediately after the war were ones of great expansion and certainty of prices with the Government urging farmers to produce as much as they possibly could to feed a nation which would have to suffer food rationing for some years to come. Prices were controlled by the Ministry of Food and for livestock farmers the emphasis was on quantity rather than quality. The whole structure of the farming industry was transformed by the Labour Government which unexpectedly ousted the great war hero, Winston Churchill. Tom Williams was the Minister of Agriculture and he, through the introduction of deficiency payments, gave farmers a sure-fire guarantee that they would get a decent return for everything they produced.

In turn the market for agricultural land was keen, particularly with capital taxation through the medium of death duties forcing many of the large landowners to dispose of at least some of their estates. The move from most farmers being tenants to a situation where the majority of them would become owner occupiers was in full swing and Andrew Oliver and Son Ltd were to benefit from it enormously.

Naturally, Ken was in the thick of the action: "At one time we had literally hundreds of farms on our books all over Britain. In fact I don't think there's a single area of the country where we haven't been involved from the Highlands and the northern half of England." The firm have even sold particular farms several times over: "Take the case of Satchells, just up the road here, I think we've sold it at least six times. Now that's what I call business."

Others to be sold included Gasbeg, near Laggan Bridge in Inverness-shire which was farmed for a number of years by the renowned farming and broadcasting character, Captain Ben Coutts. Ken remembers that sale: "We sold the 2,795 acres in 1959 for £17,300, which was thought to be a damned good price. Again in the Highlands we sold the Great Glen Cattle Ranch near Fort William to the Hon. Alan MacKay. We were told that there was 6,000 acres on the place, but I'm pretty certain there were nearer 10,000". Countless other farms were sold by the firm and of course there was very often the prospect of additional business.

"If someone wanted to buy a farm they quite likely had one to sell and we were more than willing to help with that too. Again, we were in a position to help people acquire the cattle and sheep to stock farms, and that was good for us at the mart in Hawick."

The same Alan MacKay who purchased the Great Glen was over the years to become a great friend of Ken: "In later years Alan sponsored a race at Ayr, the Joan MacKay chase, and I trained a couple of his horses - Gundagai and Musty O'Grady to win for him." Moreover, Musty O'Grady did not confine his racecourse appearances to mainland Britain: "We took him over to Ireland to run in the Galway Plate when he was ridden by Pat Taaffe, who will forever be associated with the great Arkle."

This was the first time that Ken had run a horse in Ireland and he was less than sure of the procedure regarding declarations: "I met Willie O'Grady, one of the great Irish trainers, and asked him what the form was. The next thing I knew he had grabbed me by the collar and pulled me over to a solitary official sitting at a table saying: "Here's an English bugger who wants to run a horse - put him in." Ken of course knew many Irish racing folk through his connections in the cattle trade and when they went into the paddock prior to the race he found that he had gathered an entourage of no less than thirty Irishmen, all of whom expected a measure of hospitality sooner or later!

Diversification is a popular theme in farming circles today but Ken and his father were at least a generation ahead of their time in following that path with the auctioneering business. Obviously that time in hospital during the war had fuelled Ken's imagination: "Besides buying and selling farms we were into houses and then of course we had the Kelso Horse Sales which were proving incredibly popular."

Another venture was the sale of motor cars: "After the war new cars were very hard to come by - you just couldn't go out and buy one like you can today. So we decided to hold sales in the mart on a monthly basis throughout the year. They were a great success from the start and we used to have a packed ring for every sale." Show classes for cars or *Concours d'Elegance* competitions were also introduced. At one of those events the judges were the famous racing driver Reg Parnell who drove for BRM and Berwick-upon-Tweed garage proprietor, Jock McBain who was some years later to be instrumental is establishing a young Berwickshire farmer, Jim Clark, on the road to international fame and two World Motor Racing Championships.

But in truth it was the love of being closely associated with farming that was the real driving force of Ken's life as he readily admits: "I couldn't have lived as long without being involved in all the sales we had at Hawick. We met such wonderful people - there's no doubt in my mind that farming folk are the best. I've been lucky to have known so many over all these years."

Many of those characters have now gone to tend their celestial flocks but their names live on: "I think of them all still. Arthur Elliot of Hindhope, Andrew Douglas of Saughtree, Robert Grieve of Southfield, Tom Scott of Milsington, Jasper Dodd of Riccarton, Tommy Hamilton of Earlside, Jock Inglis of Denholmhill, Bob Forrest of Preston, Tommy and Jean Elliot and oh so many more. What times we had, and indeed what stock they used to bring to Hawick."

The business of buying and selling was of course conducted in the main rings of the mart, but once the formal part was over the haven for many was the oddly named Farmers' Business Rooms or Keb Hoose. A keb hoose is very much a Border farming term relating to a pen where a ewe which has dropped her lamb before her full time might be penned up. Well, the Keb Hoose in Hawick was certainly a pen - but it was one for farmers and they often took a mighty long time to escape from it. Though, to be totally honest, very few of them showed much inclination to make that escape.

The facilities were spartan to say the least, with little more than a well-stocked bar and a few chairs and tables, but it was the company, the atmosphere and the fellowship of the farming community which made it such a special place. Sadly, the Keb Hoose is no more and much to Ken's regret: "It was a bloody shame when they knocked it down. It should have been preserved as a listed building. There's never been anything like it before, and for sure there never will be again." There are many who will testify to that, although there could be a wife or two who might have been tempted to burn it down many times. Indeed it was a place of which Robert Burns might have approved. After all it bore more than a passing resemblance to the famous tavern in Ayr where Tam o' Shanter supped with his cronies without a thought for "the lang Scotch miles, the mosses, waters, slaps and stiles, that lie between us and our hame".

But business had to come first, and in the immediate post-war period the turnover at Hawick shot up in leaps and bounds. To cope with this, a new ring was added to the mart premises and officially opened in August 1948. However, no matter how important adequate premises are, the best insurance for any auction business is good staff. During the war years the business had been carried on by Ken's father and his assistant Henry Smith who proved over many years to be a highly respected auctioneer. In late 1943 this team were joined by Ewart Inch who remained with the firm until his retirement in 1980. On the death of Henry Smith, Bob Cairns joined the team, some years later moving on to be managing director of Scotland's busiest mart in Lanark. Hawick was clearly a place to learn the auctioneering profession.

Auctioneers, however, need to be supported by a backroom team and in Jock Elliot Hawick had something different. Big Jock, as he was universally known, was a big man in every sense of the word with a rather intimidating tone of voice and a gruff manner - but a heart of pure gold. He was at one time first a bookmaker's runner and then a clerk in the days when there was a considerable business in unlicensed bookmaking. His task at the mart was to assist in the general clerking of the sales and to take the names of buyers not known to the auctioneers. In this latter operation his tone must have seemed peculiar to strangers unused to the local Hawick dialect: "Right mister, what's yer name? Eh, what d'ye say?".

His friendship was greatly valued by Ken: "He was always beside me and a great help, but really it was the character of the man and you couldn't help but like him so much, even although he could get both himself and me into some awful scrapes." One such incident involved hunter trials of which Ken was in charge: "We had a trial at Maxton, near Kelso, and I thought I would have a place where all my helpers could come for a bit of a rest and of course a drink. What happened was that the whole crowd invaded the tent and the thing became a shambles".

Following this experience he resolved to do better next time: "We had another trial at Riddell, near Lilliesleaf, and I organised that a fence would be put around the tent. But I also put Big Jock in charge with strict instructions that he was to let absolutely no-one in without an official badge." If that seemed a sound policy, then Big Jock carried it out to the letter: "Well, things were going fine, when the Duke of Buccleuch appeared and wanted to come into the tent. Big Jock said "Ye cannae get in there withoot a badge. That's ma orders frae Mr. Kenneth, but mind you if ye ask him he might gie ye a badge!"

Another famous tale of Big Jock relates to his enquiry for his boss. As was the custom in many old family businesses, the partners were referred to as Mister so-and-so. At the age of eighty-six Douglas Oliver certainly was due that measure of respect, but sadly Big Jock got things mixed up on this occasion: "See you Douglas, have ye seen Mr. Kenneth?" The old man is reliably reported to have done no more than smile.

Sadly, Big Jock did not approach the senior partner's years and died in 1960, much lamented in Hawick and further afield. "It was one of the proudest and saddest days of my life when on the morning of his funeral Jock's wife phoned me up and invited me to take a cord at the graveside. It was a real honour for me, but I lost a real friend and the whole of Hawick one of its true characters."

5

SANVINA AND JOHNNIE WALKER

Despite all the dire predictions about not being able to ride again on his return from the war, it was not long before Ken was firmly back in the saddle and thoroughly enjoying himself. Initially it was hunting which claimed his time: "I've loved hunting all my life and I've had great sport with the Buccleuch, the Jedforest, the Lauderdale, the North Northumberland, where I frequently rode Lord Joicey's horses, and the Border."

In those days after the war there was more time for everything and hunting was under far less pressure than today. "We thought nothing of hacking out twenty miles into the Cheviots to hunt with the Border for a couple of days. We would be put up overnight - invariably at Hindhope - though God knows we were never in bed because we would spend the night playing poker and having a damned good time."

One particular episode with the Border gave Ken a day he has never forgotten: "We were staying out at Hindhope with Arthur and Annie Elliot - a real husband and wife pair of characters. Well, they put me up on this little mare called Rachel and I could see from the start that she was something different because they could hardly hold her when I was getting into the saddle. In any case I wasn't feeling all that hot myself after a fairly heavy night."

Having got himself into the saddle it was off to the meet: "The meet was at nine o'clock down the road at Pennymuir. Well, when I got Rachel out of the yard at Hindhope she was off - I just couldn't stop her galloping. They had just moved away but the hounds had found a fox immediately and so we were off." It was quite a chase: "There was the fox out in front, and then me and Rachel and then the hounds. I just couldn't hold her at all no matter what I tried. We ran like blazes down over Chatto and turned again heading for Whitton Edge with Rachel never slackening." But as ever fate took a hand: "We were up on Dere Street - the old Roman Road - and heading for this big wall. She hit the top of the wall and went crashing down on her head - and that's what at last put some sense into her because afterwards she was as quiet as a lamb." Rachel went on to breed a grand line of hunters and to this day Arthur and Annie Elliot's son Tim, who was a successful amateur jockey in the 1960's and 70's, still has some of the same line at Hindhope.

Hunting in those days was more fun. There was virtually no winter grain in the Borders and Northumberland which nowadays makes hunting in arable country little more than a procession around headlands. Further up in the hills the country was well opened up and there were no mains-powered electric fences which make life sheer hell for the huntsman who knows that a sharp kick from a fence can ruin a good hound forever. But it is the company that can make even a blank day with virtually no scent still an occasion to relish and Ken had good company in plenty: "I had lots of fun with my great friend Alan Innes and of course we had Alistair Paton and we met so many people who are still friends to this day." The late Alistair Paton was truly a great man: "Alistair must have stood well over six feet six inches, yet he was the mildest of men and knew so much about bloodstock and did so much on the show circuit - including of course the Royal Highland where he was closely involved with the show-jumping."

However, Ken still hankered to get involved in the racing scene again and with a really good horse. Finding that horse, even in those days, was not an easy business but he enlisted the services of an expert: "We got a hold of Alfie Graham, who was a real judge of a horse and lived in Enniskillen. We sent him to Ballsbridge to see if he could find something that might suit me". And that he did, although there were some initial reservations: "Alfie bought this horse for £300 called Johnnie Walker from a chap called Padge Berry. Well, when the horse eventually came home to me he was lame on about three legs." That disappointment in turn prompted a visit from one of the best known horse vets of all time, Alec Tully, and he did not mince his words: "I think you've been done". Ken telephoned Alfie Graham, but he stuck by his original opinion saying: "Well, when I bought him he went round the ring as if he was on springs." A similar testimony of faith came when Ken wrote to Padge Berry who claimed that all that was wrong with Johnnie Walker was an enlarged fetlock and he would stand by the horse.

Not everyone in the bloodstock industry could be described as straight and totally honest, but after that first deal with Padge Berry Ken had complete faith in this particular Irishman: "That was the start of a long friendship. The horse turned out 100% the best hunter I ever rode, and gave me great fun as well as winning some good races. Padge and I have spoken on the telephone at least once a week ever since. No-one knows more about picking a likely young horse than Padge."

Some years later Ken was to train a horse by the name of Padge B, and he proved to be a bit of a character in more ways than one: "We ran him in a hurdle race at Kelso, but he hit the first hard and the jockey pulled him up thinking he was lame. However, he came home sound and I thought this is a bit of a soft one" Padge B was soon to disprove that notion: "We next took him to Bogside and for most of the race he was lying a long way out of his ground, but he then came home in tremendous style, winning by a huge distance." That sort of change in form was not popular with the punters and, in an obvious allusion to fellow trainer Harry Bell who was always in trouble with the stewards, there were angry shouts of "It's Oliver they want to send to London, and not Bell!"

Ken's father, Douglas Oliver, had many years of experience in dealing with Padge's father, Jack, and here too there was total trust: "Jack Berry was a cattle dealer, and my father had great faith in him and would often write to him in the days when thousands of Irish cattle were sent over to Britain and say, Jack send me over forty bullocks. He could trust him completely, and it's been just the same with me and Padge."

The first time Ken went over to meet Padge in County Wexford was, to say the least, an interesting experience: "They seemed to have some idea that I was a bit partial to the odd gin - though where they got that idea from I just don't know. But anyway, I don't think they'd ever had any gin in the house, but they produced this earthenware bottle of so-called gin which when I tasted it was more like treacle. They had poured me out a very large one, but I made an excuse to go to the loo, and when I came back I had disposed of most of it and not down my throat for once".

For a man like Ken visiting Ireland without sampling the sheer joy of hunting with an Irish pack of hounds was something that just could not be contemplated: "I hunted with Padge with the Wexford and some of the neighbouring packs and then had a day or two with my old pal from the days at Redford Barracks, Major Joe Dudgeon. I was also out with the great racing people, the McCalmonts, with the Kilkenny and had great fun with Pat Hogan and the famous Black and Tans. What days they were. Hunting in Ireland is so different. They stop at nothing and what wonderful horses they have, but you've got to be with someone who knows the country, otherwise you could get in a bit of a fix."

Another trip over to Ireland years later saw Ken travel with the Northumberland farmer, Dallas Allan, who was a great supporter of the West Percy pack. As ever it was quite a trip because Dallas Allan's zest for life was only marginally less enthusiastic than Ken's: "We were to go and see this fellow Joe Osborne about some horse that we had heard might be useful. We got lit up somewhere else with the fumes of alcohol and had to phone up and say that we would have to postpone our meeting until the next day."

On the desperate duo's arrival at the Osborne establishment they were not welcomed with completely open arms: "We were given a lecture on temperance and its benefits and told how the great jockey, Martin Molony, would come straight home from a race meeting and then sit down and read a book. Imagine that, hardly my style!" But there was more to come : "As we were leaving and going out of the door I noticed a photograph on the wall of a mare called Sanvina winning a race at Punchestown. I said to Joe Osborne - I've got that mare now, what do you think of her?" The response was distinctly unencouraging: "I don't think she's much good at all. She'll never amount to much - a pretty plain sort!" In 1950, after Ken had won several good races on Sanvina as well as reaching the pinnacle of his riding career in triumphing in that year's Scottish Grand National, he met Joe Osborne again, but this time with Tom Dreaper, the man who would later train the immortal Arkle: "It was actually at the November meeting at Liverpool, and I said to Joe - what do you think of the mare now?" Opinions do change, but the owner of Sanvina was somewhat taken aback by such a drastic change of view as had taken place in Joe Osborne's mind: "Ken my man, I thought she was a great mare - a really great little mare." And so she was, but more of Sanvina later.

The bit was now very firmly between Ken's teeth in all aspects of life and he flung himself wholeheartedly in to so many activities that it is quite astonishing that he managed to do so much and make a major success of the auction mart where, at the end of the day, he had to make his living. His lifestyle clearly proves the old adage - "If you want someone to do something, ask a busy man." Busy he certainly was. He helped to get the United Border point-to-point course at Drakemyre established, though with the track being one of the coldest places on this planet there were some who might not have particularly thanked him. He was also secretary of the Buccleuch and Jedforest point-to-point for many years as well as being secretary of the Buccleuch Hunter Trials and the Northern

Area of the Point-to-Point Association. In addition he was a Scottish committee member of the British Horse Society making regular trips to London as well as being secretary of the Trainers Federation which looks after the interests of National Hunt trainers.

Ken readily admits that without a good staff in the family business it would have been impossible to even think about being so involved. But above all he credits his father with being the most understanding of men: "He was always so kind and encouraging and in fact we were more like brothers than father and son. He gave me so much advice and even towards the end of his days we would have grand chats about all sorts of things and his advice was inevitably right."

Douglas Oliver was a man of the highest standards: "In business he taught me to always be totally straight and honest and there are many people he helped in a very quiet way, often assisting them with finance. He knew which people to back and to have faith in. I remember one farmer back in the 1930's when things were really tough. He came to my father and explained that he was strapped for cash and asked if father could help him out. He did just that by advancing some money against the sale of the first of the lambs." That farmer never looked back, nor ever forgot Douglas's kindness and today the sons and grandsons of that man are among the most progressive and successful farming families in the country. There are many more who can thank Douglas Oliver and his son for where they are today in business.

But back to racing and Ken's appetite and search for the "real good one." It is a quest in which many fail, but Ken was lucky: "I had two horses which were both lame and I was pretty fed up about this so I telephoned a great pal, Frank Hill in Gloucestershire, who was a well-known dealer and a friend of Tommy and Jean Elliot. I told him quite simply that I was looking for a horse that I could race."

Within two days Frank Hill was back on the phone: "He told me he had a decent sort of a mare and that if I didn't take her the Duchess of Norfolk would. Well, that sounded good enough for me. If the Duchess of Norfolk wanted her I had better get in quick. We agreed on a price of £350 and Frank said that he would arrange to have the mare sent up by rail as soon as he could." She duly arrived at the local station at Hassendean, just two miles up the road from Hassendean Bank, but Ken's first reactions to his new purchase was not exactly exciting: "I got her off the train at eleven o'clock at night and walked her down the road. The only thing I liked about her was that when she was walking I had to run. She looked quite dreadful, but I sent off the cheque for £350 and that was the mare Sanvina which I went on to win the Scottish Grand National with in 1950."

The ultimate success, however, was in the future but Sanvina soon showed promise and duly won on one of her early outings at Hexham - that most attractive of Northern racecourses. As ever the successful owner-jockey fancied a bit of a celebration: "We went off after the races to the George Hotel at Chollerford on the banks of the Tyne and had a real good party." It was also an occasion which led to greater things: "I had never met this character called Ernie Johnston who was a farmer and dealer, but who also had a good horse or two. It was the start of another wonderful friendship. I have always said that I met Ernie under the table, and what fun we have had over the years."

Never one to miss out on the chance of a ride on a decent horse, Ken said: "Look, Ernie, I know you've got some good horses - how about giving me a ride?" "Right, Ken, you'll get the ride on my mare Choir Belle," came the reply from Ernie whose daughter, Brenda, was years later to be one of the best point-to-point riders in the North. However, nothing happened for some time and the eager amateur was getting just a little bit frustrated: "I decided to ring up Ernie, and said to him - when am I going to get that ride you promised me after Hexham?" "Be at Leicester on Monday and we'll see what we can do."

From the Borders to Leicester forty odd years ago was not the relatively easy motorway journey that it is today, so the jockey travelled down by train: "I walked the course and had a good look at the fences because I had never ridden there before. Then I went in to collect the colours, but there had been some sort of mix-up and instead of having a red cap with white spots there was no cap at all. Well, Ernie got hold of a red cap and put the white spots on with a bit of chalk, and that was that".

The next move was out into the paddock to meet the connections, but here again fate took a hand: "I'd never met Willie Stephenson who trained the mare for Ernie, and I was just a wee bit anxious. But on the way out I met two farmers who regularly came up to Hawick to buy sheep - Fred Barnes and Alex Cullen. Well, they said to me - what sort of chance have you got, will you win?" Ken for once in his life, was clearly lacking in confidence: "I don't know about that. I think they've put a mug up today!"

In the paddock itself the confrontation took place: "Ernie introduced me to Willie Stephenson who looked me up and down - and not very approvingly at that. But he said to me with that little stutter which he always had - "this mare jumps very qu-quick, si-sit ti-tight." The race itself was a three mile novice chase and Ken soon began to understand why he had been given the ride: "We went into the first fence on the far side with three horses two lengths in front. When they took off so did the mare and we lost the lot, but I still had the mare. We went on at some pace and when I passed the stands the first time around I wondered if I was on the right course." He was and he won the race by "damned near three fences."

After the race the delighted owner, trainer and jockey went in for "some gin and tonics," and an agreement that the team should be kept together for the mare's next race the following Saturday, where she again won in a field of twenty-one runners at Nottingham. This was obviously a novice going places, but not with Ken: "You know what the devils did next? They jocked me off and put some champion called Tim Molony up! He fell off at Cheltenham." In fact Ken was the only jockey to win on Choir Belle. One report at the time said: "This mare is not an easy ride." Meanwhile *The Hawick News* reported: "The latest success of Mr Kenneth Oliver, the Hawick amateur rider, was his win on Choir Belle at Nottingham on Saturday. In winning a great race Mr Oliver defeated the noted Molony brothers." One racing correspondent described it as 'the finest exhibition of racing and jockeyship seen this year.'

However, the friendship was well forged: "I had tremendous fun with Willie and his wife Bobbie and one day I was given a ride on a horse of Bobbie's at Huntingdon. I said to her - Bobbie, there's one thing I'll do for you. I'll make a bloody good show for you." He certainly did: "I fell off the horse in front of the stands. Willie was not pleased, but Bobbie and I got stuck into the champagne and he just cleared off and left us to it." The saga was not over yet: "We drank champagne for a good while, but eventually it came time to head for home. We got outside and into the car but we couldn't move for traffic. We were stuck in a right jam and we knew that Willie would not be too pleased if we were late home."

Nothing daunted, the famed Oliver ingenuity came into play: Ken said, "Bobbie sit still as a mouse and don't say a word. Next I waved at this policeman and wound down the car window and said to him - look we've got a problem here, my wife is going to have a baby, can you please let us through? We got through without difficulty after that!"

Another major influence on Ken was Stewart Wight who trained at Greenwood, near Grantshouse on the Berwickshire coast: "He was probably the best trainer of all time in Scotland and did so much with limited material and opportunities. He trained over 1000 winners in forty years and was simply a marvellous man to know and work with. He tried his best - and I could never have achieved any success I did without his help to teach me how to ride a race properly. He always had time for amateurs and when you think of all who learned the game under Stewart it's a measure of the man."

That list is a roll-call of some considerable honour in the annals of National Hunt racing - Reg Tweedie who rode Venturesome Knight for Stewart Wight to be fifth in the 1940 Grand National and who was later to saddle Freddie - second in the National in 1965 and 1966. Reg Tweedie later became chairman of Kelso Racecourse and was behind the inauguration of the race which commemorates his former master.

Ken remembers many more of those pupils: "There was Major Ewan Cameron who rode over eighty winners and later went to be a leading figure in National Hunt racing as a member of the Jockey Club. Then there was Adam Calder who bred that wonderful horse, Flying Ace, who won over fifty races with his daughter Doreen riding." Ken always followed Flying Ace's record breaking career with particular interest: "I must claim a small part in that success. Adam asked me if I knew of a nice mare to breed National Hunt horses. Well, I had a little mare called Flying Eye by Vulgan who found the fences just that bit too much for her with 12st. 7lbs. on her back, but she was a good sort and she certainly proved her worth for Adam with Flying Ace."

Ken clearly enjoyed those days and the friends he made. "Among the others to pass through the 'Stewart Wight School' were Danny Moralee who went on to be a very good jockey, and we cannot forget Fulke Walwyn and Frank Furlong - they came down from the barracks in Edinburgh to ride out most mornings in the early 1930's." Indeed not, for Frank Furlong rode Reynoldstown to win the National in 1935 while Fulke Walwyn's turn came the next year when he took the same mighty horse to victory.

Stewart Wight, as Ken recalls, was a hard taskmaster: "You had to do things right for Stewart and if you didn't he would give you a right telling off. He was known as 'Bossy Wight' but two minutes later he would be having a gin with you. He was that sort of a man and I've always wondered how he would have done if he had been training in the south. I think he would have been among the very best - he knew so much about horses and how to handle them no matter how difficult they might be. Stewart was undoubtedly the person from whom I learned so much."

Similarly, his appreciation of Reg Tweedie is enormous: "Without a doubt if Reg had been riding today he would have been the top amateur year after year. He was quite brilliant, but apart from that he and his wife

1950. Ken and Sanvina winning the Scottish Grand National at Bogside.

1955. J. J. Paterson, Peggy Paterson, Ken and his father at the Auction mart at Hawick.

"Teviotdale Farmers 125th Anniversary Dinner, 1981."

Standing: Stuart Oliver, Walter Grieve, Fraser Morrison, Charles Scott and Ken.

Seated: Lord Gray (Minister of State for Agriculture), Dan Buglass (Author), Alastair Hutton (M.E.P.)

1952. Cheltenham National Hunt Festival. Ken is to the rear in the spotted colours at the first flight on his way to victory in the Birdlip Hurdle.

1959. Bechers second time. The moment before Tim Brookshaw's stirrup iron broke.

1960. The Melleray Belle's Challenge Cup at Ayr – Wyndburgh beating Kerstin, the Gold Cup winner.

The early 1960's. Crossing Denholm Bridge towards the village.
Wyndburgh and Rhona, Sanlace and Willie Lauder, Berrycleugh and George Hogg,
Honeytown and Ken.

c.1966. Hunting with the Buccleuch. Three Grand National heroes – Winnie Wallace on Meryman II, Rhona on Wyndburgh and Ken on Mr. What.

Betty have bred an awful lot of good horses which have done well for other people." In more recent times it is Reg Tweedie's work at Kelso which means even more: "He's done so much for Kelso and built its reputation to the point where it stands near the top today. Just look at those fences - there's not a stiffer finish anywhere in the country and that's why we've seen so many horses go on from winning at Kelso to win or do well at both Cheltenham and Liverpool."

That high praise for Kelso is by no means biased for a few years ago racing journalist, Martin Trew, when writing for *The Times*, conducted a survey of each and every racecourse in the country awarding them jockey's caps on a scale of one to five. Only two received top marks - Sandown and Kelso. Both racecourses became firm favourites with the Oliver stable when Ken eventually took out his trainer's licence.

Ken was always, in his own terminology, 'a bit of a devil for punishment.' On one occasion he hunted for a full day - and a full day was just that - before driving to Edinburgh to play in a squash match, returning that night and then driving to Stewart Wight's to ride out. But that was not the end of it: "I went off to Doncaster after that and rode a winner." No-one to this day has been able to fathom just where his energy comes from, but it is still there.

But it is time to return to that famous little mare, Sanvina, and her quite extraordinary influence on the entire racing scene. Truly this mare has been one of the outstanding racehorses and brood mares of her generation and even now, over forty years after she won the Scottish Grand National at Bogside, her influence is as strong as ever.

As Ken recounts she was not an impressive new arrival at Hassendean Bank and when she was sent to Stewart Wight he was not impressed, especially after her comparative failure on the point-to-point circuit: "I think we'll enter her in a seller and then get rid of her and buy you a decent horse." However, under the tutelage of the Master of Greenwood Sanvina gradually began to improve and when the time came for her to run in the seller at Perth he had changed his mind: "I think we'll keep the mare, she might be better than we thought."

But Ken was not so sure: "What if she wins the seller?" Stewart Wight came back with a quick and definite reply: "We'll buy her in, that's what we'll do." Considerable discussion followed with Stewart Wight having his way up to a limit of 400 guineas which Ken thought was quite mad. Sanvina duly won "very easily" with Jimmy Power, who had won the 1950 Grand National on Freebooter, in the saddle, but the crunch was to come when the auctioneer asked for bids because even Stewart Wight was beginning to regret ever running her in the race. However, she was duly bought for 160 guineas. "Thank God," says Ken who had been unable to make the trip to Perth on account of a large sheep sale at Hawick: "She proved to be a great ride for me and tremendous fun always."

Much fun was had along the way winning races at Kelso, Carlisle and Hexham on the way to Bogside for the big race. Despite these modest successes Sanvina was definitely an outsider.: "We started at 66-1, but more importantly we were set to carry 12st. 2lbs., a great weight to carry round for four miles at Bogside which was a far stiffer test than the race at Ayr nowadays. Memories of the actual race are still crystal clear: "At the second fence in front of the stands, which had quite a drop, she pecked badly on landing with the result that my wrist was bent backwards. But that was probably the best thing that could have happened because it knocked her back a bit and got her to settle."

Gradually the mare got her wind and made up ground towards the last where "we were absolutely flying and there was no chance of anything passing us." A report in one of the next day's papers described Sanvina as "winning like a five furlong sprinter." Celebrations would normally have been very much in order for the successful owner rider, but Stewart Wight intervened: "Now remember I want you for the last race, so behave yourself."

For once the advice was heeded and Ken went off to the ambulance room to seek treatment for his injured wrist: "It was bloody painful and beginning to swell, so I was given pain-killing injections. However, word had got around the racecourse that Oliver was well away and on his third bottle of champagne." In consequence Ken's mount in the last, his own Johnnie Walker, which should have been a firm favourite, drifted in the betting with the money opting instead for one ridden by the well-known English amateur, Atty Corbett. The two reached the last stride for stride but Ken had plenty in reserve: "I was sitting there with a double handful and I shouted across to Atty - come on let's make a race of it." However it was not to be and Johnnie Walker coasted home a very comfortable winner. Johnnie Walker was something of a character, rather like his owner: "Padge Berry used to say that there wasn't a better hunter in Ireland and that he was almost human. In fact Padge told me that he would say 'Johnnie, it's time you had a new set of shoes', and off he would go to the blacksmith, get shod and come back on his own."

Ken had enormous enjoyment with Johnnie Walker in the hunting field and qualified properly, not as some today who "just turn up at the meet and trot up and down the road for twenty minutes." Following his success at Ayr the programme was to take Johnnie Walker the next season to both Cheltenham and Liverpool for the Foxhunters. However, the plans went awry on the very last day's hunting in the best of the Buccleuch's hill country near Selkirk when Johnnie Walker hit a stone wall rather too hard and had to be boxed home immediately. It was to be a race against time: "He should have gone to Stewart Wight but that wasn't possible, so my good friend Bobby Fairbairn came over every day to Hassendean Bank from St. Boswells to try and get him sound. In the end we got him to Stewart and ran him in a preparatory race at Sedgefield."

It was a race too soon: "We were leading into the last but he fell, completely exhausted." Stewart Wight was determined that another race was still necessary so it was off to Birmingham: "I was bang on the rails and brought down at the second fence, so we ended up at Cheltenham, definitely not as well prepared as we would have wished." The Foxhunters at Cheltenham is a race dear to the heart of all amateurs and Ken was keen to win it: "I led into the last, but the hill took its toll and we had to be content with second place." Disappointment indeed, and ironically the winner was a horse called Greenwood - the name of Stewart Wight's farm!

Liverpool was next on the agenda and here Johnnie Walker was installed as favourite. It is a day etched forever in Ken's memory: "Johnnie cantered down to the start quite the thing, but then he saw a white starting gate and stuck in his toes with the result that I ended up on the ground! He looked down at me with a look that could only have meant - you silly old fool, for heaven's sake get up." The going at Liverpool suited Johnnie Walker and he pinged both Bechers and the Canal Turn but then fate took yet another cruel turn: "I looked behind me and saw nothing in sight. There was only one in front but we were just cantering two lengths behind on the outside as we came to Valentines and then the other horse ran right across me, fell and brought me down."

Nothing daunted, Ken was determined that this was not to be the end of his race: "With my short legs I was never very good at getting on to a horse, but I saw a policeman attending to the other jockey and shouted 'for God's sake leave that bugger and give me a leg up!'" Mounted again Ken and Johnnie Walker flew over the remaining fences and finished third. Johnnie Walker's last race was at Manchester and sadly it ended in tragedy when he fell at the water and broke his back. Ken was shattered and to this day the memory of it brings a tear to his eye: "I lost a very dear friend that day who gave me so much pleasure. There was never another like him. Poor Johnnie." A dislike of water jumps has remained with Ken ever since and no-one was more pleased than him when his local course at Kelso did away with the water in front of the stand in 1990.

But back to Sanvina. After her win at Bogside she went on to win a few more races but sadly she suffered minor leg trouble and it was decided to breed from her. Ken sent her to Ireland to Padge Berry: "Thereafter she had three filly foals in succession - and they were all right ones." Indeed they were, for two of them subsequently won on the same day at Kelso while the other one was placed third - again on the very same day - at a point-to-point. Those Kelso winners were Melgund Glen and Honeytown and this latter one in particular proved herself time and time again. She stood only fifteen hands but being by Fortina she never lacked for courage, although a certain lady rider - Rhona Wilkinson - of whom we shall hear much more later, got a nasty scare in Honeytown's first point-to-point at Friarshaugh, Kelso, when she ran into the rails after the last with the race at her mercy.

Later Honeytown ran in novice chases including a two mile event at Bogside. Tim Brookshaw was the jockey and he clearly had mixed views on his mount for at the start he was heard to ask the other jockeys: "Have you ever ridden a bloody two-year old in a novice chase before?" Yes, she was small, but she won that race in style. Honeytown and Tim Brookshaw were less lucky on another occasion at Bogside - this time in the Scottish Grand National - they were brought down at the third last when "going tremendously well."

When she went to stud Honeytown really came in to her own and to date she has bred the winners of no less than fifty-three races under National Hunt rules. Among her offspring have been The Benign Bishop, Chandigar and Ballyowen who won five consecutive races in Ireland when trained by Padge Berry for Ken. However, perhaps the best of them all is one of modern day racing's real heroes - Deep Sensation, bred from a daughter of Honeytown, Bannow Bay, and trained so patiently by Josh Gifford.

The tale behind Deep Sensation is one that gives Ken great satisfaction: "I sold the horse as a yearling at Doncaster in 1987 for the then record price of 23,000 guineas to Timmy Hyde who brought him back again two years later but passed him out unsold. However, I got hold of Josh Gifford and persuaded him to buy the horse privately." It must be one of the best buys of the shrewd Gifford's life for to date with the best still surely to come Deep Sensation has won over £250,000 in prize money.

Two of those wins came in the spring of 1993 and they brought enormous pleasure to both breeder and trainer. The first came in the two mile

Queen Mother Champion Chase at the Cheltenham Festival meeting. The seemingly unbeatable Waterloo Boy was hot favourite but Deep Sensation, showing a resolution that many had doubted existed, left the field for dead. On television after the race, John Gifford said: "Apart from winning the Grand National with Aldaniti, this is the biggest thrill of my career as a trainer. This is a really good horse." Back home in Hassendean Bank Ken had watched the race from his armchair and was "so proud that the tears were running down my face." Shortly afterwards Deep Sensation did it all over again at Liverpool winning the Martell Chase and stamping himself as possibly one of the most exciting chasers for many years as well as seeing Ken being recognised as "Breeder of the Month" in March 1993 by the Thoroughbred Breeders' Association.

Ken is convinced that it all goes back to Sanvina: "She was a good mare on the track but her offspring are quite fantastic - they have shown that they can win at any distance from two to four miles."

Honeytown's half sister, Melgund Glen by Scottish Union, also promised much according to Ken: "She was a beautiful horse, and the idea was to win a novice chase with her and then send her back to breed from with Padge Berry." She was a good second in her first novice chase at Newcastle and then went on to Catterick: "It was a day when racing should never have started due to the gale force winds and sadly she was one of the five horses killed that day. It was an absolute tragedy - but that's racing." Indeed it is, and everyone involved in racing must accept that.

6

ENTER RHONA AND WYNDBURGH

The Grand National is one of the world's greatest sporting spectacles. It is much more than just another steeplechase. It is the supreme challenge for both horse and rider and to compete over the thirty or so Liverpool fences is a dream close to the heart of every jockey. For most just to jump Bechers, swing around the Canal Turn, meet Valentines in full flight, cross back over the Melling Road and then face up to the Chair in full view of the packed grandstands, never mind a worldwide television audience, is a thrill which can never be forgotten or substituted. Old men who rode in Grand Nationals fifty years ago still get a gleam in their eye at the very mention of the world's greatest race.

To own or train a National winner is to have a passport into the history books of National Hunt racing. However, in the purely Scottish context, it is a race which has proved singularly unlucky. Time after time a Scottish horse has come tantalisingly close only to fail, until at last, in 1979, Rubstic made it a truly Scottish triumph. Rubstic was trained at Bedrule just over the River Teviot from Hassendean Bank, by John Leadbetter, who at one time worked in the Oliver yard. The lucky owner was former Scotland and British Lions rugby star, John Douglas, while the jockey was the Cumbrian, Maurice Barnes.

Nobody was more pleased for John Leadbetter than Ken and Rhona. They knew how hard John had struggled with his small yard to find owners and decent horses and of his faith in Rubstic when others said he was less than genuine. However, as they enjoyed John's moment of glory, their thoughts inevitaby returned to the one horse which had come so close for them so often in the past and of how fate had dealt them a different hand. That horse was Wyndburgh. He was something special and although he never stood in the winner's enclosure at Aintree his place is secure in the National history.

Sporting heroes come with all sorts of pedigrees and even in this day and age spending a fortune is no certain passport to success. Wyndburgh's beginnings could hardly have been more humble, but as so often is the case, there was one man who had an eye open to some hidden potential. It all began not long after the war in the mart at Hawick when a local farmer, Major P.C.E. Wilkinson, bought a mare for his young daughter Rhona. Rhona, besides being determined to be a farmer, was fast outgrowing her pony and was beginning to show a distinct inclination to try her hand on the Northern point-to-point circuit.

Rhona remembers it vividly: "Father went to Hawick Mart one day and bought a mare from the Robson Scott Family for literally not much more than knacker price. The idea was that I should use her for riding round the sheep at home". The second mare, the dam of Idlewood, was bought a few days later from the knacker yard at Carlisle and kept as a brood mare. In his day Major Wilkinson was regarded as one of the best farmers in the district and always had that special quality in knowing stock. To use the local vernacular, he was "a guid kenner". His insight probably never reaped a better reward than the purchase of those mares, but then again, perhaps Major Wilkinson knew full well that the Robson Scotts had bred sound stock for generations.

Shortly afterwards Rhona went off to an agricultural institute - "they call them colleges now" - and it was decided that the mares should be put in foal. The mare who was to leave her mark was called Swinnie, after a farm high in the Jedforest country where many a good day's hunting had been enjoyed. The chosen stallion was Maquis who stood at Midshiels Farm in the charge of young Harry Bell and his father. Maquis' stud fee was a modest £25, but he came from true blue blood, with his sire being none other than the 1938 Derby winner, Bois Roussel. The mating was certainly no high-powered deal. Swinnie had cost just £18 and together with the stud fee, the end result for the grand sum of £43 in the early spring of 1950, was an under-sized colt named Wyndburgh - so called after a hill south of the town of Hawick. The rest is history, but one cannot help but wonder how the reputation of Maquis might have soared had he not met with an unfortunate accident. All of his progeny to run under Rules were winners.

In the spring of 1953 when Wyndburgh was three, Rhona realised she had a problem. "I had broken several young horses myself, but I soon came to the conclusion that this one was different. Although he wasn't a very big horse, he was much too strong for me". Professional help was required and it was to Bobby Fairbairn's livery yard at St. Boswells that Rhona turned. Bobby knew a good horse when he saw one and in later years proved this point time after time when he set up as a trainer near Selkirk. He turned out a whole host of winners from there, amongst which African Patrol and Tamerosia are best remembered. Bobby and his assistant Willie Shiel, certainly did the trick with Wyndburgh and were impressed enough with the youngster to venture the suggestion that "he should be tried over hurdles".

Rhona and her father accepted Bobby's suggestion and in the early autumn of 1954 Wyndburgh was put into training. As a four/five year old he ran six times in the 1954/55 season. Wyndburgh never finished in the first four of any of these races and it would be unfair to say that he showed more than a glimmer of promise. It was therefore decided that he would not go back into training the next year but that Rhona would hunt him and ride him in point-to-points. By the time Wyndburgh had turned six he was a very much better horse than when he had appeared over hurdles. He and Rhona ran twice and were placed both times. By now Rhona's father had taken out a permit which allowed him to run both his own horses and those of any unmarried daughter under Rules proper. For some obscure reason, now long forgotten, having been run in point-to-points Wyndburgh was put back to hurdling and in early April, 1956 ran in a handicap hurdle at Carlisle with his usual lack of distinction.

Wyndburgh's next outing that season was in a hunter chase at Kelso when he ran with great promise and finished second to a very useful horse of Ken's called Kickim, ridden by Roddy Bamber. Danny Moralee was on Wyndburgh. Kickim was named by Ken after Willie Stephenson's habit of saying to his jockey in the paddock, with his slight stutter, "k-k-k-kick 'im in t-t-the b-b-belly".

By 1956 Ken had virtually retired from the pigskin and taken out a permit to train. Prior to his marriage to Rhona Ken's best horse was Duncormick, bought from Padge Berry and named after the village where Padge was living at the time. Another horse which Ken ran under permit and which also came from Padge was The Boss Man.

The next time Wyndburgh ran was at the May Meeting at Cartmel, when he won a novice chase over three miles, £300 added. In retrospect it was a fairly undistinguished race, but Wyndburgh won it by a distance. Significantly this win qualified Wyndburgh for entry to the Grand National.

After his win at Cartmel Wyndburgh was turned out for the summer.

Obviously he must have got up in late July as his next appearance was at Sedgefield on 15th September when he ran unplaced. On 27th September he won a three mile chase at Perth at 20-1. He continued to improve and ran nine more times, winning on four occasions and being second three times. The Mayfair Chase was run on 15th December, 1956 at Hurst Park and Wyndburgh travelled south for it, coming fourth to Dick Francis riding Crudwell. Dick had a bad fall at Newbury the next month and this was one of his last wins before he retired from race riding.

In the autumn of 1956 Rhona was away with the other horse which she trained. As stated earlier her father held the permit, (women not being allowed in those days to hold licences or permits by the Jockey Club). The Wilkinsons lived a mile and a half on the Carlisle side of Hawick and Ken at Hassendean Bank, five miles on the Kelso side of Hawick so she asked Ken to exercise Wyndburgh. He was impressed with the horse and with his uncanny ability to judge a horse's potential by riding it or just looking at it, he told Rhona that in his opinion Wyndburgh was a National type of horse. As a result of this advice and due to Wyndburgh's win at Cartmel which qualified him, he was duly entered for the great race in early 1957, although aged only seven.

After Hurst Park Wyndburgh's next race was at Ayr. He came fourth and followed this with the four-and-a-quarter mile Tote Investors Chase at Newcastle on February 16th. Ridden by Mick Batchelor (his regular jockey, Pat Morgan, could not do the weight) and carrying 10st. 4lbs. he won, making him a live candidate for the world's greatest steeplechase. The Tote Investors Chase was sponsored by Tote Investors, so it would appear the commonly held view that the Whitbread at Sandown was the first ever sponsored chase is factually incorrect. The Tote Investors Chase is a recognised Grand National trial.

His win at Newcastle did Wyndburgh no favours with the Grand National handicapper, as he was set to carry 10st. 7lbs.. If he had fallen or been unplaced in the Tote Investors Chase he would not have been given more than 10st. or 10st. 1lb.. Those six or seven pounds were to prove vital. In an attempt to stop falling attendance, the day of the big race had been put back to a Friday and it was run on 29th March, 1957. Wyndburgh was 33-1 and the two most strongly fancied horses were Goosander at 5-1 and Much Obliged at 10-1. It was a very good calibre field including two previous winners in E.S.B. and Royal Tan, and the Gold Cup winner, Four Ten. Amorial III took the lead, but went at the fourth when the running was taken up by the enormous Sundew, ridden by Fred Winter. Sundew led for the rest of the race and although he made a number of diabolical mistakes which would have unseated lesser jockeys than Fred, he kept galloping on through the deep which he loved. After the second last The Crofter challenged, but was soon spent and Wyndburgh, who had always been within twenty lengths or so of the leader, ran on to be second, beaten eight lengths.

1957

POSITION	NAME	JOCKEY
1st	SUNDEW	F.T. Winter
2nd	WYNDBURGH	M. Batchelor
3rd	TIBERETTA	A. Oughton
4th	GLORIOUS TWELFTH	B. Wilkinson

By anyone's standards Wyndburgh had run a great race and perhaps if he hadn't won that race at Newcastle and had had six or seven pounds less in the plate, he would have made a real race of it with Sundew. As it was the winning post came too soon. Incidentally, the last seven-year-old to win a Grand National was in 1940 when Bogskar owned by Lord Stalbridge, beat the eight-year-old MacMoffat, owned by Captain L. Scott Briggs.

Wyndburgh put up a couple of smashing performances after his Grand National run. Firstly, he won the Grand Sefton on 9th November over two miles and seven furlongs (the shortest race he ever won) around the Grand National Course, again ridden by Mick Batchelor. As a result of this he was immediately installed as favourite for the next year's race. After Christmas, Wyndburgh returned to Newcastle to run in the Tote Investors Chase and won it once again. This win ensured he was a raging hot favourite for the National.

For the 1958 Grand National Wyndburgh was allotted 11st. 7lbs.. When the tapes went up on Saturday March 29th, he was a strong favourite at 6-1, with Goosander at 100-7 second favourite. Once again ridden by Mick Batchelor Wyndburgh lay within striking distance of the leader Goosander (ridden by Tim Molony) for much of the race. At Bechers Mr. What took over the running, followed by Goosander, Tiberetta, Eagle Lodge, E.S.B., Green Drill and Wyndburgh. As they crossed the Melling Road Mr. What was ten lengths ahead of his rivals and, ridden by Arthur Freeman, was thirty lengths ahead of the second horse, Tiberetta, as they crossed the line. Wyndburgh improved his position a bit after Bechers and finished fourth, although he was beaten a very long way. In retrospect Rhona thinks he was probably a little unfit as she was training him on his own and he was getting lazy with nothing to work with.

1958

POSITION	NAME	JOCKEY
1st	MR. WHAT	A. Freeman
2nd	TIBERETTA	G. Slack
3rd	GREEN DRILL	G. Milburn
4th	WYNDBURGH	M. Batchelor

The most important event in Ken's life that year took place on 6th May 1958 when he and Rhona were married. Best man at the wedding was the great hunting enthusiast, Jimmy Hogarth, over whose farm at Mosshouses, near Galashiels, the Lauderdale Hunt have held their point-to-point each May since the fixture was moved from neighbouring Blainslie, where Ken had ridden his very first winner - the one-eyed Delman. After the wedding Rhona brought her horses up to Hassendean Bank and these of course included Wyndburgh. When he re-appeared at the start of the 1958/59 season Wyndburgh's owner was now Mrs. J.K.M. Oliver and he was trained under permit by Mr. J.K.M. Oliver.

A plan of campaign was mapped out by the newlyweds for the 1958/59 season. The three main targets were the Grand Sefton at Aintree, the Eider at Newcastle and then back to Aintree for the big one. Fred Winter was given the mount in the 1959 Grand Sefton and rode one of his few injudicious races. After the last he tried to squeeze up as they came to the elbow on Jimmy Fitzgerald's inside. Jimmy, who was still claiming, quite rightly shut the door and by the time Fred had checked Wyndburgh and came on his outside, Jimmy on Polished Steel had gone, so once again he finished second over the Liverpool fences. Rhona's mother died so Wyndburgh missed the Eider which, as it turned out, was abandoned due to snow and frost, but they took him down to Warwick to run in the Warwickshire Chase. As Tim Brookshaw was claimed to ride E.S.B., the ride was given to a young nephew of Willie Stephenson, David Nicholson. Now commonly known as 'The Duke', David is one of the top trainers of jumpers in the land, with a superb training establishment at Jackdaw's Castle in the Cotswolds. David steered Wyndburgh to victory under 11st. 2lbs. but nearly collapsed when he came to unsaddle as he had had his appendix removed only a few weeks earlier. As Ken remarked, "they made them tougher in those days".

It was a great occasion at Hassendean Bank when the time came to leave for Aintree, as it was the first time Ken had trained a runner in the race. All the staff both from the farm and Andrew Oliver & Son Limited were there to wish them luck and to give the team a rousing send off. Ken says of the day: "Just for luck we decided to take big Jock Elliott from the mart with us as our mascot and give him some entertainment in appreciation of all his hard work and encouragement. He was a real Wyndburgh enthusiast". Also making the trip was George Hogg, Ken's head lad.

Tim Brookshaw was taking over the ride on Wyndburgh from Mick Batchelor and was set to carry 10st. 12lbs., a reduction of 5lbs. from the previous year. For once the betting proved a sound indication of the horses' merits as at the off they went: 6-1 Mr. What, 8-1 Oxo, 9-1 Slippery Serpent and 10-1 Wyndburgh. The bookies just about got it right as three of the four favourites filled the first three places.

The field went off at a merry pace the lead alternating between Surprise Packet with Gerry Scott up and Tiberetta ridden by Alan Oughton. Surprise Packet fell at Bechers second time round and just behind him came Oxo and Wyndburgh. As they landed, Tim's offside stirrup, not the leather but the actual iron itself, broke. He quickly kicked his other leg free and joined issue with Michael Scudamore on Oxo. A tremendous battle ensued with first one horse half a length up and then the other. No greater feat of horsemanship has ever been witnessed at Liverpool. Odd as it may seem, as they raced over the fences Tim called out to Michael on Oxo, "What shall I do, what shall I do?". At the time a very popular tune was, *Does your chewing gum lose its flavour on the bedpost overnight?*, so Michael turned in the saddle, patted his bottom as if sticking on a piece of chewing gum and replied, "use your ******* chewing gum!!" This can clearly be seen from the film of the race.

Not unnaturally the strain of riding virtually bareback started to tell on both Wyndburgh and his jockey and Oxo pulled ahead on the run in to the last fence. He was probably about four lengths up when he hit it hard and nearly fell. It was a remarkable feat of jockeymanship that Michael stayed in the saddle, but stay there he did. At the elbow Oxo was three lengths ahead, but coming to the end of his strength. Tim on Wyndburgh must have seen or sensed Oxo's tiredness and under an inspired ride got Wyndburgh to within a length and a half of Oxo at the line. If the run in had been another 400 yards, Tim and Wyndburgh, even without irons, would have been at least a length and a half in front. Oxo was trained by Ken's great friend Willie Stephenson. "Willie was among the first to commiserate with us and people like Fred Winter and Neville Crump - the masters of Liverpool - all said that we would have undoubtedly won but for that awful quirk of fate".

That, of course, is all part of racing, but the newspapers the following day were almost more full of the courage of Tim Brookshaw and the sheer bad luck of Wyndburgh than they were of Oxo's win. Indeed, watching a replay of the race more than thirty years later one cannot fail to be amazed at the way in which Tim Brookshaw stayed with the horse and of how he came so tantalisingly close to victory. All the valiant jockey said after the race was: "I'll be a bit stiff to milk tomorrow". He truly was a sportsman as well as a great jockey.

1959

POSITION	NAME	JOCKEY
1st	OXO	M. Scudamore
2nd	WYNDBURGH	T. Brookshaw
3rd	MR. WHAT	T. Taaffe
4th	TIBERETTA	A. Oughton

This century there have been four *really* unlucky losers in the Grand National. There can be no doubt that the unluckiest of them all was Devon Loch, owned by Her Majesty Queen Elizabeth the Queen Mother, and ridden by Dick Francis who has since done so much to keep the tradition of the Grand National going and is now a Trustee of Aintree. Devon Loch's collapse some fifty yards from the line remains one of racing's great unsolved mysteries. Devon Loch was a clear winner that day and if Dick could have got him going again after he sat down, he was still far enough in front to have won. Devon Loch was trained by the later Peter Cazalet, as was Davy Jones, who came to the last in the 1936 Grand National with the race at his mercy, ridden by the Hon. Anthony Mildmay (later Lord Mildmay) when his reins suddenly parted and he ran out. The other two horses who had really bad luck were both Scottish and their losses were also due to saddlery failure. In 1930 Melleray Belle's iron broke and she was only beaten a neck by Shaun Goilin, the same fate as Wyndburgh suffered.

As a direct result of Wyndburgh's run in the 1959 Grand National Ken took out a Licence, mainly to train a horse called John D. owned by Senator J.D. Sheridan. The first winner which Ken had as a fully licensed trainer as opposed to a permit holder, was on 2nd December, 1959 when Wyndburgh won the Christmas Cracker Chase at Liverpool over the Mildmay course, ridden by Fred Winter.

The first race he won for an owner outside the family was on 5th March, 1960 when John D. went in a novice hurdle at Kelso - twenty-five ran. Obviously still very much the star of the stable, Wyndburgh's main objective remained the Grand National.

The 1960 race was run on 26th March and the handicapper raised Wyndburgh's weight from 10st. 12lbs. in 1959 to 11st. 7lbs., the second highest weight carried that year. The top weight was Mr. What. The favourite at 13-2 was another horse from the Buccleuch country who had also run in point-to-points, Merryman II, owned by Ken and Rhona's friend, Winnie Wallace. He was set to carry 10st. 12lbs. Wyndburgh was second favourite at 8-1 and was now at about his peak as far as the National was concerned, being aged ten. Wyndburgh was ridden by Michael Scudamore, the previous year's winning pilot, but gave him no chance when he hit Bechers hard first time and Michael shot over his head. Wyndburgh didn't actually fall although nine horses out of ten would have done. Merryman, ridden by Gerry Scott, won easily by fifteen lengths.

1960

POSITION	NAME	JOCKEY
1st	MERRYMAN II	G. Scott
2nd	BADANLOCH	S. Mellor
3rd	CLEAR PROFIT	B. Wilkinson
4th	TEA FIEND	P.G. Madden

Ken's first season as a public trainer finished with four wins supplied by three different horses. However, in the same way that Tim sensed Oxo was coming to the end of his strength in the 1959 Grand National, the racing world sensed that the Hassendean Bank team, with Ken overseeing and placing the horses, Rhona acting as his assistant trainer and chief work rider and George Hogg as head lad was a winning one, and the number of horses in the string quickly expanded. Wyndburgh was their first winner of the 1960/61 season when on 15th October he won the

Melleray Belle Cup at Ayr by a length, ridden by Gerry Scott and beating the Gold Cup winner, Kerstin, with Stan Hayhurst up.

In the 1961 Grand National, Tim Brookshaw once again had the mount on Wyndburgh and was set to carry 11st. 5lbs.. Excluding the Russians who weren't handicapped so were given an automatic 12st., Merryman II carried top weight with 11st. 12lbs., second top weight with 11st. 8lbs., was Oxo and Wyndburgh was third top weight. The Irish horse, Jonjo, ridden by the legendary Pat Taaffe was 7-1 favourite, followed by Merryman II at 8-1. Wyndburgh was half neglected in the betting at 33-1.

Wyndburgh was close as they jumped Bechers the second time, but from then on the leaders drew away from him. In fact it was an exciting race, with Merryman II and Nicolaus Silver racing together until the second last at which point the grey, Nicolaus Silver, pulled ahead to win by five lengths. He was ridden by the Irish jockey Bobby Beasley and trained in Worcestershire by Fred Rimell. Wyndburgh finished sixth.

1961

POSITION	NAME	JOCKEY
1st	NICOLAUS SILVER	H.R. Beasley
2nd	MERRYMAN II	D. Ancil
3rd	O' MALLEY POINT	P.A. Farrell
4th	SCOTTISH FLIGHT II	W. Rees

The going in 1961 was very fast and Wyndburgh had always been a better horse on the soft, if not on the deep. By now he definitely did not need fast ground so he ran a very good race and wasn't beaten more than thirty lengths. Often in those days a horse could be 3rd or 4th in the National if he managed to get within thirty lengths of the leader. It is perhaps worth noting that Nicolaus Silver's time was just over 9 minutes and 22 seconds, while Sundew took exactly 20 seconds longer in 1957, when Wyndburgh was second for the first time.

Ken and the team at Hassendean Bank finished the season with sixteen winners - a big increase from the four he had in his first season as a public trainer and it was obvious that he was going to be a major force to be reckoned with, not only on the Northern racing circuit but throughout the length and breadth of the British Isles. A Ken Oliver trained horse was soon respected when it appeared at Southern tracks such as Sandown, Ascot, Kempton or Newbury; by now Hurst Park had departed from the calendar.

At the start of the 1961/62 season Wyndburgh was getting a bit old in racing terms at the age of eleven, so it was decided to have one last crack at the National in 1962 when he would be twelve. As usual the preparations were immaculate and Wyndburgh seemed to be as keen as ever, "pulling like blazes", when Rhona rode him out at exercise.

The jockey for this final crack at the race was one of the real characters of the Northern racing scene, Cumbrian farmer Tommy Barnes, whose son Maurice rode Rubstic to win the National in 1979. Tommy Barnes had ridden several winners for the Oliver stable and Ken had great respect for him, both as a jockey and as a man: "We had him booked one day to ride for us on a very hard pulling horse called Union Jackson at Catterick. Before the race Tommy had taken a very hard fall and it turned out he had broken his collarbone. However, Tommy rode our horse to be second". After the race the mettle of the man was to emerge. "I said, 'Tommy. How's your shoulder?' All he said was, 'It grates a bit. I think I will have to see the quack' and that was after riding a race with a broken collar bone!"

As the Liverpool meeting approached, Ken realised that Tommy had never even been to the course before, far less ridden over the famous fences, so it was thought prudent to give the pilot some preliminary instruction. It was decided to give him a ride in the Topham Trophy over the National fences on the Thursday, on a little grey horse called Brief Sparkle. The combination duly completed the course without getting into a place, but the purpose had seemingly been served. As they unsaddled Ken and Rhona got something of a surprise when they asked Tommy how he had coped with the fearsome Bechers Brook. "Which one was that?", he asked in his thick and unmistakable Cumbrian accent, and then "Is that the one at bottom?"

But there was more to come. On the Saturday morning when they all met up on the course Rhona showed Tommy a copy of *The Scotsman* newspaper with a massive photograph of Brief Sparkle at Bechers doing everything but completely fall over. The legs were splayed out and the horse's head was almost tucked underneath his chest. "I thought you had got on fine at Bechers - what's all this about?". Tommy was as ever brief with his retort: "Oh, aye, he did oop arse a bit at one." It was obvious that he had little idea of where the famous fence was on the course when he added: "Aye, Bechers, that be down at the bottom end, is it not?" Still, on the great day, Tommy Barnes was to prove himself more than equal to the challenge.

The going at Aintree on 31st March, 1962 was deep, if not very deep. The weather was variable, with spells of sunshine intermixed with driving hail and sleet. The two favourites were Frenchman's Cove at 7-1, Solfen at 9-1, followed by Nicolaus Silver and Kerforo at 100-9. None of the four fancied horses in the betting finished in the first six and the race turned into a contest of stamina. At Bechers second time two Irish horses led the field - Fredith's Son and Gay Navaree. These were followed by Mr. What, Wyndburgh, Nicolaus Silver, Clear Profit and Kilmore. The winner had to come from this group. The four left in the running as they jumped the second last were Gay Navaree, Wyndburgh, Mr. What and the improving Kilmore. These four horses raced to the last virtually in line. Kilmore touched down a length clear of the other three. Fred Winter and Kilmore soon showed their dominance and within 100 yards of the last fence were three lengths clear of Wyndburgh, who in turn was a couple of lengths clear of Mr. What. At the line Kilmore was ten lengths in front of Tommy and Wyndburgh who were the same distance in front of Johnny Lehane and Mr. What. Gay Navaree and Mr. Tony Cameron ran on to be fourth. Kilmore was trained at Findon in Sussex by Ryan Price.

1962

POSITION	NAME	JOCKEY
1st	KILMORE	F.T. Winter
2nd	WYNDBURGH	T.A. Barnes
3rd	MR. WHAT	J. Lehane
4th	GAY NAVAREE	Mr.A. Cameron

That was Wyndburgh's last race, but he lived on for well over twenty years more - for over half of that period brilliantly carrying Rhona to hounds. Rhona says of him, "Even in his twenties he could pull your arms out and make your shoulders ache".

As an individual Wyndburgh was certainly not the slashing, great chaser represented by such horses as Golden Miller, Prince Regent and Mill House. These were the *beau ideal* of many followers of the Winter game and the type of thoroughbred of which the sporting artist Snaffles would have said, "Carry a man and 14st. 7lbs. slap bang over Leicestershire or Limerick or 12st. 7lbs. round Liverpool if asked". Wyndburgh was nearer 15.3 hands than 16 hands and to look at him one would have thought 12st. 7lbs. would have been quite enough for a day's hunting. The great

Scottish trainer, Stewart Wight, said of Wyndburgh early in his career, "Well, I don't think he is any more than a good hill hunter"; although after Wyndburgh's second win at Perth he did agree that perhaps he had been wrong and Wyndburgh would in fact make a racehorse.

Although small to carry 12st. or 12st. 7lbs. around chase courses, Wyndburgh was a nice individual with a beautiful, intelligent, all quality head, lovely shoulders and good heart room, but for a racehorse he was decidedly shortcoupled (i.e. had rather a short back). In many ways he is reminiscent of Vincent O'Brien's great little horse Hatton's Grace, who won three Champion Hurdles, an Irish Lincoln over a mile and an Irish Cesarewitch over two miles. Neither horse was big, but both were 'hammered together' - a complimentary phrase used by horse dealers to mean a horse is well made and will wear. As it happens, both Wyndburgh and Hatton's Grace ran good races at the age of eleven or twelve and lived to a healthy old age. Both were as brave as lions and although certainly very un-prepossessing in the paddock, were great favourites with the racing public for their ability and above all their determination.

If Wyndburgh was not Snaffles' idea of a perfect thoroughbred, certainly Lionel Edwards fell in love with him. In most peoples' opinion Edwards was best as a sporting artist when depicting the countryside with hounds crossing it and on the whole his commissioned portraits of individual horses are far from his best work. However, his oil of Wyndburgh with the hills in the background must be one of the best, if not his actual best, commissioned study of a horse. Wyndburgh could be termed as the ideal woman's horse and to misquote Snaffles one could say of him, "he would have carried 12st. slap bang over Leicestershire or the Buccleuch and 11st. round Badminton if asked".

As a racehorse, Wyndburgh had many of the attributes of a great horse. Firstly he was durable and ran at least five times for eight consecutive seasons. Secondly, he jumped well and thirdly, right until the end of his days, after many hard races, he always ran his race out to the end. He was a rare horse in that he was certainly better over four or four-and-a-half miles than three or three-and-a-half. He was a very useful staying chaser and around Liverpool over the big Grand National Course he was a good horse. If that stirrup iron had not broken at Bechers in 1959 Wyndburgh would have won that Grand National and gone down in the history books not just as a good horse, but as one of the all-time greats of Liverpool.

7

TOP SCOTTISH TRAINER

Wyndburgh retired after the 1962 Grand National, having come second for the third time. Since then, over a period of more than thirty National Hunt Seasons, Ken and Rhona have proved that they have run one of Scotland's most successful public National Hunt Stables. However, Ken says that "undoubtedly the greatest Scottish National Hunt trainer this century was Stewart Wight. He had over a thousand winners and there was a lot less racing in his time and travel was far more difficult. If he had runners at Wetherby or Hexham on a Saturday, they had to leave by train on the Thursday, while nowadays they are there and back in a day".

The Oliver stable has always concentrated on chasers. This is not surprising taking into account Ken and Rhona's hunting and point-to-pointing background. In fact it would be fair to say that picking up races over hurdles was a bonus for most of their horses before they began their more serious careers over fences. As we shall see, they have had a few top class hurdlers.

Ken has always favoured the horse specially bred for jumping, the type of horse which quite often doesn't mature until he is seven or eight and is not seen on a racecourse until he is five or six, rather than the flat bred horse. Naturally, as in anything, it is always the exception that proves the rule and one or two of Ken's best horses were either flat bred or had run on the flat before going to Hassendean Bank. Ken's best horses came from three main sources: Padge Berry, Doncaster Bloodstock Sales (where he bought two Scottish Grand National winners in Fighting Fit and Cockle Strand) and the horses which bred Ken himself, principally from the Sanvina line.

It is not the authors' intention in this chapter to give a blow by blow account of all the big races won or lost or the good horses trained, as this is a general biography of Ken Oliver the man and not just the trainer. The Appendix at the back of the book lists the best twenty or so horses which have been stabled at Hassendean Bank together with a brief description of their breeding and major triumphs. No book about Ken could deal with, however briefly, all of his successes and heartbreaks in the thirty-one years since Wyndburgh retired.

Ken had in George Hogg as head lad one of the very best. It was much more than just a working partnership. "George was a grand chap and he knew so much about horses and how they were in themselves, and that isn't something that you can really teach anyone. They either have it or they don't and George certainly had. Ken and George had known each other since the point to-point days, but things did not always run smoothly for George. "He farmed with his father, but when the old man died George wasn't left very well off and had to quit the family farm. Then he went to Stewart Wight as a shepherd during the war". From the Grantshouse stable George moved on as stud groom to Alistair Paton, before arriving eventually at Hassendean Bank. At first he looked after Ken's horses as well as being involved with the farm; but when Ken took out a full trainer's licence, George was very much the head lad.

George was always a man who enjoyed nothing better than a day out at Kelso and very often he had a few drinks. Some people may have considered he had one too many, but not Ken. "George was totally dedicated and would walk here from the village at any time of the day or night to see to the horses. He never took holidays as such, so he was perfectly entitled to have the odd day out. He certainly enjoyed himself and knew a lot of people. He was also a great judge of a horse and truly knew how to feed, but above all he was very loyal".

George could also size up a potential stable lad very quickly and assess if he was up to the job, but staff were never a problem for Ken: "We always seemed to be very lucky. I think that was down to the fact that the town of Hawick and the surrounding district is horse mad on account of the Common Ridings, with the result that we were never short-staffed". Another factor was that for a number of years in the sixties and seventies the Borders became a sort of mini Lambourn or Malton, with three relatively successful yards close together and the lads all knew each other.

Some of those stable lads inevitably got into a variety of scrapes. Peter Ennis, who developed into a useful jockey with a win in a Scottish Grand National on Young Ashleaf, was very often the instigator. One night after a dance in Jedburgh while the lads were walking the five miles home to

Hassendean Bank (no buses ran at that time of night) the bold Ennis removed a garden gate. Unfortunately for the gang, the local constabulary had been hidden observers of the misdemeanour. Their tactics were admirable and Ken agreed with the instant justice. "The police waited until they got home and then they bundled them into a van, took them all the way back to Jedburgh, made them replace the gate and then told them to get walking!"

Just a mile or so up the road was the farm of Midshiels where Harry Bell trained. Harry was always something of an enigma to the rest of the racing world. There is no doubt that he was a great judge of a horse and could always place a moderate animal to win a race. Distance was no object to the Bell yard. Harry himself was a considerable gambler and had many a hefty coup, but it was said of him that he wouldn't even tell his own mother if he thought one of his horses was going to win, far less the owners.

Harry Bell achieved considerable success over a quarter of a century, including three Scottish Grand National winners - Quick Reply in 1972, Sebastian V in 1977 and Astral Charmer in 1981. Furthermore, Sebastian V was only just touched off by Lucius in the 1978 Grand National. Unfortunately Harry was forever in trouble with the authorities and made several visits to the Jockey Club headquarters in Portman Square, in addition to having countless brushes with the stewards at meetings all over the country. To say he resented authority and being told what he could and could not do would be an understatement. Eventually, and very sadly, he ended up in Jedburgh Sheriff Court on a charge of causing unnecessary cruelty to a mare and was sentenced to six months imprisonment. It was a sad end to his career, but few of the people who knew Harry and his black moods were all that surprised.

The other local stable, and a much happier place, was at Over Whitlaw, near Selkirk, where Bobby Fairbairn had his yard. Bobby had a lifelong passion for horses and was of course associated with the making of the young Wyndburgh. From having a small livery yard in the village of St. Boswells, Bobby was lucky enough to have the backing of the wealthy Misses Robertson of the Cutty Sark whisky company, whose patronage was invaluable to Scottish racing over many years. Bobby rewarded their faith with a string of winners, as well as scoring for a long list of other owners. Those days were a golden period for Scottish racing and as Bobby Fairbairn's widow and daughter, Ethel and Barbara, remember: "They were happy times and while we were all out to get the winners, Bobby and Ken would be among the first to congratulate each other after a win". The rivalry between the three stables was friendly but intense. However, Ken Oliver was the king, although later he was to acquire a nickname which has stuck to this day - The Benign Bishop.

As stated elsewhere, one of the reasons that Ken took out a full licence rather than continuing to train under permit, was that Senator J.D. Sheridan had asked him to train for him. The Senator provided Ken with his first winner for an outside owner in John D. Another horse which he had in training with Ken in the early days was a chaser by the name of Pappageno's Cottage. In his first year, Pappageno's Cottage won a small novice chase at Perth ridden by Tim Brookshaw who afterwards remarked to the trainer, "I think he's just a moderate selling plater". It also appears that Senator Sheridan thought this racing business was getting too expensive for him (he had a long-standing reputation of being extremely cautious in his financial dealings) and so the horse was sent for sale at Kelso in 1961. Trade that day was mixed and Pappageno's Cottage was let out unsold at a mere 420 guineas, but that was far from the end of the story.

When he had finished selling, Ken headed for the bar to catch up on the day's gossip. "There I found two of the drunkest men I think I have ever seen - John Sheridan and this fellow Willie King who was involved in several businesses, including a hotel and cattle dealing. The pair had a deal and Willie was the new owner for 500 guineas". At least the horse was sold and hopefully he would stay in the yard, but that was not Willie King's intention. "He told me that he was taking him home to hunt and that he couldn't afford our training fees".

Rhona then took a hand: "The pair of them were so drunk that I took the horse home and eventually persuaded Willie that he should run him in a race at Carlisle in which we had already entered him". Pappageno's Cottage duly won that race and set sail on a highly illustrious career which culminated in that Scottish Grand National triumph in 1963 with Tim Brookshaw, who had by then revised his opinion of the horse, in the saddle. Sheer delight was the reaction of owner Willie King who had "a fair gamble", all the way down from 50-1 to 20-1, never mind lifting the richest prize in Scottish jump racing.

Due to the weather, 1962/63, the season after Wyndburgh retired, was the hardest the British Isles has known since 1947/48 and Hassendean Bank, like the rest of Britain, was basically under snow from Christmas until early March. There was only one race meeting held during that time which happened to be at Ayr. The Oliver string had a marvellous training ground on the Minto Hills, just over a mile away from the yard, and it was on those hills that Ken and Rhona exercised their string virtually every day during that bitter weather.

It was a hungry time: "We couldn't run the horses anywhere, but at least we kept them fit. Mind you, such was the severity of the winter that the dogs which were out on the hills with the horses could catch the foxes. I have never seen foxes so lean as they were in 1963". The reward for all those frozen hands and icy feet came at Cheltenham in March, with the great freeze breaking just in time for the meeting to go ahead.

Happy Arthur was installed as 4-1 favourite for the George Duller. Ridden by Tim Brookshaw, and carrying 10st. 8lbs., he quickened from two out and won easily by eight lengths. In January, 1964 Pappageno's Cottage won the four mile Fred Withington Chase, ridden by Swannie Haldane who was one of the real characters of the weighing room. John Swanston Haldane, or Swannie to everyone, he was a local lad who Peter O'Sullevan once described as having "the shortest and bandiest legs in racing". Swannie came to Hassendean Bank after Stewart Wight's retirement and while he had a great love of horses and riding, his new master found it less than easy to persuade him to help with more menial tasks. He was and still is a right character, but when a load of straw or hay arrived you could be absolutely certain that no trace of Swannie would be found until the unloading was over.

On the strength of 'Old Pappa's' win in the Fred Withington, he was set to carry 11st. in the 1964 Grand National and was installed as one of the four joint favourites at 100-7, along with Laffy, Time and Flying Wild. The great Pat Taaffe, who was regularly employed by the Olivers in the sixties, took the mount, but he didn't run a particularly good race and finished a well beaten tenth to the winner, Team Spirit.

The following season Pappageno's Cottage went down again to Cheltenham in early January 1965 for the Fred Withington and once again won it, the successful jockey being Terry Biddlecombe. In March the same year the Olivers won their first chase at the Festival when Lady Edmonson's seven-year-old, Fort Rouge ridden by George Milburn, won the Grand Annual over two miles.

Two really top class horses made their appearance from Hassendean Bank the next season - Arctic Sunset and Even Keel. Arctic Sunset's owner was the great Scottish racing enthusiast, Jimmy McNair, who farmed at Musselburgh, near Edinburgh. He counted himself very lucky to own a horse like Arctic Sunset and never failed to dip into his pocket after a good win.

Arctic Sunset came over to Scotland having won his only two races for

Paddy Sleator in Ireland. In November, 1965 he won a novice chase at Newcastle as he liked, and then slammed a goodish field when winning the Henry VIII Chase at Sandown. His third in in a row was at Cheltenham's National Hunt Festival when he won the two mile Cotswold Chase for novices (now the Arkle). In all of these races he was ridden by George Milburn.

In the 1966/67 season Arctic Sunset won the Supreme Novice Chase at Haydock and ran a marvellous race, again at the Festival, when he was third in the Two Mile Champion Chase, now The Queen Mother Champion Chase. He looked as if he would be a Cheltenham Gold Cup horse in 1968, having run second over two and a half miles in the Mackeson in November, but he was tragically killed at Sandown in January, 1968. Not only was Arctic Sunset a really top class horse with aspirations for the 1968 Cheltenham Gold Cup, he was a lovely individual in the stable and to ride. Ken himself used to ride him out most mornings.

Even Keel, also made his appearance for the Olivers during the 1965/66 season but unlike Arctic Sunset, he didn't set the world alight that season. It wasn't until the next year when he won five hurdles on the trot that people realised what a good horse Even Keel was. In all he won twenty-three times. Ken has saddled a whole host of big race winners over the years and near the top of that list must be Even Keel. "A great horse who was a real crowd pleaser. His jumping - when he was on form - was quite spectacular."

Even Keel was a horse who frequently showed his best form in the south, winning the Benson & Hedges Gold Cup and Express Chase at Sandown, as well as the Kirk & Kirk Chase at Ascot.

The previous season another youngster had made his debut from Hassendean Bank. Although like Arctic Sunset and Even Keel he was full of ability, alas it was flawed ability. That youngster was not a horse, but a young Irish jockey by the name of Barry Brogan.

On the night of Barry's arrival at Hassendean Bank in October, 1965, Ken and Rhona took him to a party at Douglas Elliot's farm at Middletoun. It was, like all of Douglas' parties, a boisterous affair, but Ken had warned the raw eighteen-year-old: "Now look here Brogan. I'll do the drinking for both of us!" Barry heeded the bidding on that occasion but it was one of the few times when he did. Ken had been warned about Brogan: "Tom Dreaper told me that he was something extra special, but that I might not like the bit extra".

Barry was soon riding winners for Ken at a prodigious rate and attracting rave notices, suggesting that in time he might well become a champion jockey. He was a great judge of pace and possessed an astonishing drive in a close finish. Undoubtedly he won races on horses that other jockeys would have lost, yet he was never too hard on the horses. Over a period of years on the Northern circuit there was intense rivalry between Barry and another young thruster, Brian Fletcher. Brian was also getting the winners. Indeed he went on to ride two Grand National winners, first on Red Alligator in 1968, and then his name really entered the history books when he rode Red Rum to the first of his never to be forgotten triumphs in 1973 and again in 1974. When Brogan and Fletcher were riding against one another it was possible to sense something more than just the atmosphere of the race. It was a contest between the two to prove who was better.

Barry Brogan has often been compared to the footballer George Best, and with due cause. They both had so much talent, yet they both wasted gifts with which very few are blessed. Drink and gambling brought about the downfall of both of them, although a fondness for attractive female company also played a part.

After settling in at Hassendean Bank, Brogan began to find his way around the local nightspots. The pubs in Denholm were usually his first port of call and then very often he would be off to the Tower Hotel in Hawick where his easy charm soon made him the centre of attraction and the recipient of copious quantities of alcohol. Thereafter there was no holding him back. Frequently he would scarcely be fit to ride out in the mornings, far less to ride in an important race, but his constitution was truly amazing and time after time his fellow jockeys in the weighing room would be astounded to see what they regarded as "a pissed Brogan" ride yet another winner.

Ken and Rhona knew full well what was going on, but as Rhona ruefully remarks: "He was headstrong and you could tell him nothing. He would pour his heart out to you one day saying that he was finished with all the boozing and the carrying on, but the very same night he would be back at it again".

Despite all the winners which Brogan rode for Ken relations inevitably became less cordial: "One day Barry appeared in the house and said that he had been offered a retainer to ride for Fulke Walwyn. I wasn't all that surprised and told him that I wouldn't stand in his way although I advised him against going south. I thought it would be the end of him".

Ken was right in his judgement. True Brogan did win a King George VI Chase at Kempton for Fulke Walwyn on The Dikler, but the bright lights and bad company beat him. He fell foul of the big gambling schools, ending up by being banned by the Jockey Club for three years. Worse was to come with a year in jail for a theft which had been fuelled by his twin obsessions of gambling and alcohol. He then wrote his autobiography in which all sorts of claims were made about many people in racing, although he obviously respected the Olivers and on the whole spoke well of them. Ken says, "He ended up a real bad egg. It was such a pity because I hate to see anyone wasting talent". Ken's old friend and great rival Arthur Stephenson perhaps summed it up best of all: "I warned you about him when he first started to ride for you. He can get the winners when things are going well, but he needs watching". Unfortunately no-one could ever watch Barry Brogan all the time.

Wolverhampton Racecourse is a very long way from the Borders and it is not a course where, in all honesty, many trainers particularly seek to run their horses, but in the story of Ken Oliver that course holds a very special place. History was made there one day in 1968. November 11th was the date and it was to prove a different sort of remembrance day for the Hassendean Bank stable with five runners and five winners - and a five-timer for stable jockey, Barry Brogan.

The raw facts are recorded for posterity in the form book, but as ever with Ken there is far more to the tale than just turning up with five horses: "It all started with a horse called Drumikill, another from Padge Berry. Rhona was very fond of the horse which belonged to an old friend called Stewart Black who used to have horses with Stewart Wight. Rhona told me she had found a likely race for Drumikill after searching the racing calendar and that it was at Wolverhampton of all places".

Ken's reaction rather shocked his wife. "Wolverhampton be damned. I am not going near that bloody awful course again". Then the story came out. "After the war when I was riding as an amateur and keen to get rides, I was riding the odd horse for a chap in Cumberland by the name of Jack Pearson who had had the odd brush with the stewards in his time. One day I was riding a horse for him at Wolverhampton, and coming round the final bend he swerved to the outside. In the end I finished second, well beaten by at least ten lengths". That, however, was not the end of the matter: "Next thing I was up in front of the stewards and accused of not trying. Me, not trying, I ask you!!"

Jack Pearson gave Ken his only winner as a jockey at the National Hunt Festival. "On Monday (3rd March 1952) Jack rang me and asked if I would ride a horse of his called Dankali in the Birdlip Selling Hurdle at the Festival on the Wednesday. He had 11st. 10lbs. and had been running promisingly, so he had more than half a chance. Obviously nobody turns down a ride at the meeting, especially with the chance that Dankali obviously had". But Ken was in for a shock. "I changed into Pearson's colours as he was owner/trainer of the horse and went into the paddock. There was no-one there except the lad who was leading the horse around. Dankali looked as if he hadn't been groomed for a month, his mane and tail hadn't been brushed out and he had the dirtiest rug I have ever seen and that was hanging down one side and trailing along the ground. I can only assume that I was given the ride as they wanted to have a major gamble. Anyway, he opened at 5-1 and was backed down to 7-2 second favourite".

"At the post Dankali stood quite rigid and I honestly thought that I would get left at the start. He did jump off just behind the others as can be seen from the photograph and we jumped the first flight just about last. He was a super ride and we challenged the leaders coming to the last and went on to win by four lengths. A horse called Michael Collins ridden by George Stack was second and Rouge et Noir, ridden by Fred Winter, third. Also behind me were my friends Tim Molony and Bryan Marshall". Ken asked to ride the horse again, but was never given the chance, fuelling his pre-race impression that he had been put up on Dankali to confuse the betting market.

Anyway, Rhona, undaunted by Ken's misgivings over Wolverhampton, was determined and got together a team of five horses for her chosen fixture. Ken, Rhona and Barry Brogan travelled to Birmingham to stay the night, but first, Rhona says, "We stuck Brogan into something like an incinerator to get him dried out so he would he half fit for the morning". Certainly Barry rode brilliantly. His first winner was in the first race which he won on Glenkiln. There were no Oliver runners in the next three races. The fifth race, yet another novice chase went to the Olivers and Barry when Even Keel won, although he hit the last two hard and had to be ridden out. The sixth race, the Nuneaton Hurdle, was the most valuable on the card and Drumikill got home by a length from Nothing Higher, ridden by David Nicholson. Thanks mainly to Barry's inspired riding, the next race fell to the Oliver runner, Ballycurragh Lad, despite a number of mistakes made by the horse which would have unseated many a lesser jockey.

With four winners under the Olivers' belt one of the party, the Hon. Simon Fraser, son of the great war hero Lord Lovat, had to go back to London for an important business meeting. As he left he said to Ken: "If Shingle Bay wins the last I stand to win at least £7,000 from my original investment of £75 (now £70,000 to £750)."

The excitement was mounting by the minute and it was certainly getting to the owner of the last of the stable's quintet, Mrs. Agnes Ogilvy, the wife of a prominent lawyer from Edinburgh. It was one of those days forever etched in Ken's memory: "Agnes really was a wonderful lady and full of fun, but this time she had had perhaps more than her fair share of the Scotch. Anyway, there was a field of twenty in the race and so poor Agnes made her way across the paddock - and certainly not in a straight line - to Shingle Bay where she gave Barry Brogan a most affectionate kiss and wished him the very best of luck". Seldom was a jockey so fondly despatched.

Shingle Bay must have also taken note for he won his race handily, returning to scenes of great rejoicing. Agnes was delighted, but as she was leading her horse to the winners enclosure she stumbled and fell and the horse fell over her! Fortunately neither horse or owner were any the worse and the entire crowd joined in the fun - the dour folk of the Midlands were unaccustomed to such frivolity.

Back home in the Borders the local punters had a field day and the tale went the rounds that one of the Hawick bookmakers was seen late at night with a rope around his neck. The Wolverhampton winners were duly commemorated in a fine oil painting which hangs at Hassendean Bank, while Simon Fraser invested some of his winnings in a horse which he named, unsurprisingly, Wolverhampton.

That same season Drumikill was a really good hurdler and nearly sprung a great surprise in the 1969 Champion Hurdle. Rhona says of him: "He was a funny horse. He went faster in the deep than he did on good going". March 1969 opened with torrents of rain and it kept on raining right up until the Cheltenham Festival, which opened on Tuesday the 18th of March. On the first day the going was so incredibly deep that the Gloucester Hurdle (now the Trafalgar Supreme Novices Hurdle) was run at nearly thirty seconds above the average time. As always the big race on the second day was the Champion Hurdle. Persian War was 6-4 favourite and the only other horse which was seriously fancied was the great L'Escargot, who was to go on to win two Cheltenham Gold Cups and a Grand National. He loved the deep and was backed down from 8-1 to 11-2 second favourite.

Despite the extremely deep going, the race was ridden at a smart pace, with the field being taken along by the confirmed front runner, Bobby Moore, who led for the first five flights. Supermaster then took over until the sixth, where he gave way to Drumikill whose last three races had all been won on the soft. As they came to the last it was Drumikill a length to the good being driven ferociously along by Barry Brogan with Persian

94

War under the utmost pressure from his pilot, Jimmy Uttley. It was any-one's race. The bookies were screaming "Take two to one". However the race was lost at the last. Drumikill virtually missed it while Persian War put in a smashing jump and was away and gone before Barry could get his mount back into his stride. At the post Persian War was four lengths in front of Drumikill who was two and a half lengths in front of Privy Seal.

Before going on to Ken's third decade as a public trainer, a brief mention must be made of yet another high class staying chaser which he trained, the giant Moidore's Token. In his day he was an above average staying chaser, but he ran the race of his life when it mattered in the 1968 Grand National. Here he finished second ridden by Barry Brogan to the Brian Fletcher ridden Red Alligator. Moidore's Token never got a blow in at the winner and was in fact probably lucky to beat the Peter Cazalet trained, David Mold ridden, Different Class by a neck for third place. Different Class was owned by the popular film star, Gregory Peck. In fact Mr. Peck had, some four or five years previously, bought Pappageno's Cottage only to have him fail the vet. If he had passed, he would have stayed with the Oliver yard so they just missed having Gregory Peck as an owner. The best horse which Gregory Peck had was the grey, Loving Record, trained by Tom Dreaper to win the Leopardstown Chase.

The Spaniard, together with Drumikill, was the best hurdler to run from Hassendean Bank. He was a very good juvenile hurdler and won the important Lancashire Hurdle at the Grand National Meeting in 1966. His other major win was in the George Duller in 1968 at the Festival Meeting when he carried 12st. 2lbs. to victory, giving at least 7lbs. to all the other runners. Although George Milburn had said of him early on in his career when schooling him over hurdles, "this horse will never jump, but he will always get to the other side", he became a very useful chaser in the season 1969/70, winning three of his last four races including the Scottish Grand National in 1970, which by that time was run at Ayr, having been transferred from Bogside in 1966.

Scotland's greatest chase fell for the third time to Ken in 1971 when the great staying mare, Young Ashleaf, won it. Young Ashleaf's career is covered in some detail in the Appendix. Tommy Stack, who often rode Young Ashleaf and was later to team up with Red Rum to win a Grand National, said of the horse: "I still believe to this day that she was a great little mare. She wasn't very big, but she was one of the best horses I have ridden and also one of the unluckiest, so often meeting a horse that was better handi-capped on the big day". Young Ashleaf was particularly unlucky when she came second in the Whitbread at Sandown. She was also second in a Hennessy at Newbury.

The late Peter Cazalet trained Her Majesty Queen Elizabeth, The Queen Mother's horses at Fairlawne in Kent with Jim Fairgrieve as his head lad and right hand man. Jim was a good judge of a horse and bought quite a few, including some highly successful ones, for the Cazalet stable at Doncaster Sales.

The Queen Mother held Jim in great esteem, as he had played a big part in her many winners, particularly once Peter Cazalet's health started to deteriorate. In 1973 Fairlawne closed down on Peter Cazalet's death. Jim and his wife Dora wanted to return to Jim's native Scotland and Peter's son, Edward (now the High Court Judge, Sir Edward Cazalet, Q.C.) had a bungalow built for them on the banks of the Tweed at Birgham near Kelso.

The Queen Mother was keen that Jim's involvement with her horses was continued and sent Earls Castle to the Olivers on Jim's recommendation. Later Jim bought Burning Bush for Her Majesty in Scotland and both he and Earls Castle won races for the Olivers. On Jim's death Her Majesty sent a superb wreath to the funeral. Over the years Jim became a close friend of Ken and Rhona and gave them much valuable help and advice.

In the early 1970's one of Ken's good servants was a horse he bred himself, The Benign Bishop, which he gave to his son Stuart. He was a really nice chaser, winning on sixteen occasions and being placed on another ten. The Benign Bishop's two best wins were in the Welsh Champion Chase at Chepstow and the Scottish Novice Champion Chase at Ayr. The Benign Bishop is a name which has stuck to Ken. Indeed there is a highly revealing photograph of him, seated on something akin to a throne, his eyes firmly closed in slumber and dressed in bishop's robes.

At the Annual Jockey and Trainers Dance at the George Hotel in Penrith, by the early hours of the morning Ken was having a well deserved snooze. Liz Barry (wife of the famous jockey, Ron) and Beryl McCain (Ginger or "Red Rum" McCain's wife) dressed him up in ecclesiastical garb much to the amusement of the rest of the party. All in all it must have been a good night as Dorothy Squires was heard to remark that dancing with Ken was like having a sauna. Unfortunately she had failed to notice that one of her shoulder straps had detached itself!

Ken, however, says this is not how he got the nickname. He says it came from an article in *The Field* written by Tim Thompson, once clerk of the course at Doncaster, which basically said, "...If one was to visit Hassendean Bank one is met by a distinguished, small, slightly rotund

1960. Kelso. John D. flattens the last before becoming Ken's first winner for an outside owner.

1961. Galloping – Rhona on Wyndburgh and Ken on Honeytown.

1961. Melgund Glen (left) and Honeytown (bottom) winning the two divisions of the Crailing Novices Hurdle at Kelso, ridden by Nimrod Wilkinson.

1962. November. Happy Arthur and Nimrod Wilkinson winning the Bob Wigney Handicap Hurdle at Cheltenham. He went on to win at the 1963 Cheltenham Festival.

1963. Mr. W. King leads in Pappageno's Cottage,
having won the Scottish Grand National
at Bogside.

1967. Barry Brogan on Fort Rouge sailing over the first before winning the Childers Handicap at Doncaster.

1967. Robert Irving, Arctic Sunset and George Hogg at Hassendean Bank.

103

1969. The Cheltenham Festival. Drumikill making a mistake at the last flight in the Champion Hurdle, while the winner, Persian War, jumps it fluently.

figure, who one would think was a benign bishop and not a leading race-horse trainer". We present the evidence in photographic form in this book of the first story and the reader can take his or her choice as to which version is true.

If that wonderful day at Wolverhampton was a one-off experience in Ken's life there were many more great times, not the least of which was the day when another horse from this upstart stable in the North won the much esteemed Hennessy Gold Cup at Newbury in the autumn of 1979 with Fighting Fit: "We had some owners from Hexham - Tom Carr and his wife, lovely people who knew a bit about racing. Anyway, they wanted a horse and came down to Doncaster for the May sales but there was nothing to suit them. They said that they would come back for the June sales. I said there was nothing in the catalogue puntable, but they decided they would come for "the beer" anyway. After the sale was over we went into the bar where we met an old friend of mine, Major Hugh Delmage. Hugh was a great amateur rider in Ireland and subsequently became Steward of the Irish Turf Club. He liked to come to Doncaster, to see if he could buy something to turn over. In the past he had bought and taken a small profit. I asked Hugh if he had bought anything. His reply was, 'Ken, I can't believe it. I've bought a lovely horse for 2,000 guineas'. I went out to see him and fell in love with him straight away. I must have missed him in the catalogue. I asked Hugh how much he wanted for him and he said, 'just give me £250'. That was it. The deal was done and I passed him on to the Carrs. A great day's work done." That horse of course was Fighting Fit who went on to win the Hennessy and the Scottish Grand National in 1979.

The last winner of the big Ayr race for Ken was Cockle Strand, ridden by David Dutton, and while all winners give the yard a lift, this one was just that bit special. "He belonged to one of our best supporters of all time, Colonel David Greig, who has done so much for Scottish racing and to win at Ayr for David really pleased me immensely".

In fact the plans were set long before that victory and Ken proved to be a highly accurate tipster. "I was the auctioneer and when Cockle Strand came into the ring at Doncaster I announced 'this is the horse that will win the 1982 Scottish Grand National'. "It was a bold prediction, but that 18,000 guineas investment by Colonel Greig was one that was warmly greeted in the winner's enclosure at Ayr where he has served in a variety of positions, including that of joint chairman of the racecourse. That particular Scottish National was also memorable, because Ken's other runner, Three To One, ridden by Jonjo O'Neill, finished second to Cockle Strand only beaten a neck. The Greig colours are still active and despite his advancing years the owner is frequently at Hassendean Bank to ride out his own horses. Friendship and respect was forged many years before between owner and trainer: "David is one of the old school of racing people and we could do with a lot more like him today. I have never known anyone who has ever said a bad word about David Greig".

In 1984 Ken bought a very nice grey three-year-old by Precipice Wood who, when named High Edge Grey, developed into a first class chaser, best remembered, like Even Keel, for his spectacular jumping. Unsurprisingly, being by an Ascot Gold Cup winner, High Edge Grey needed time and it was not until the 1988/89 National Hunt season that he really came good. He started off by winning a couple of nice races at Kelso and then won the highly prestigious Charlie Hall Memorial Pattern Chase at Wetherby in November. Taken south to Newbury, he started favourite for the Hennessy, but slipped up on landing two strides after the fourteenth fence when going easily. High Edge Grey will always be one of Ken's favourite horses as he carried Ken's grand-daughter, Sandy Forster, to a win at Kelso on her first ride under Rules Proper in February 1991.

It is interesting to hear Ken and Rhona reminisce about their long and successful partnership in training some of the best National Hunt horses which many of us have had the pleasure to watch for well over thirty years.

As can be seen from the table following during the seasons 1967/68 to 1971/72 (inclusive) Ken was consistently in the top ten.

TRAINER	HORSES	RACES WON	VALUE £
1967/68			
Denys Smith	26	55	37,944
T. F. Rimell	34	69	25,801
P. Cazalet	28	56	23,195
A. R. Turnell	17	30	22,921
W. A. Stephenson	33	70	22,794
H. R. Price	27	43	21,650
C. H. Davies	10	17	20,822
K. Oliver	25	56	18,153
F. Walwyn	23	45	15,256

(Continued)

F. Cundell	22	42	14,898
F. T. Winter	21	37	14,581
K. Cundell	13	22	14,024

1968/69

T. F. Rimell	32	62	38,444
G. Balding	22	42	32,760
F. Walwyn	36	54	31,301
W. A. Stephenson	33	61	25,134
H. Price	24	33	21,178
G. W. Richards	16	30	19,693
C. H. Davies	15	30	18,602
F. Cundell	22	47	18,554
K. Oliver	23	49	17,561
F. T. Oliver	19	41	17,323
P. Cazalet	24	45	16,399
N. Crump	19	41	16,304

1969/70

T. F. Rimell	35	77	61,864
W. A. Stephenson	43	114	49,121
F. Walwyn	28	56	31,418
F. T. Winter	25	53	31,011
K. Oliver	25	56	29,496
P. Cazalet	20	42	26,415
D. Barons	32	66	24,931
C. H. Davies	22	36	21,913
N. Crump	16	33	21,671
Ryan Price	23	30	21,263
Denys Smith	23	54	20,683
R. Turnell	18	31	20,429

1970/71

F. Winter	29	73	60,739
T. F. Rimell	37	72	49,080
W. A. Stephenson	52	110	44,749
R. Turnell	21	48	32,113
K. Oliver	26	56	31,098
G. W. Richards	22	52	30,952

(Continued)

J. E. Sutcliffe	6	59	26,114
F. Walwyn	27	47	21,748
P. Cazalet	18	34	20,839
D. Gondolfo	27	57	20,217
H. Thomson Jones	20	35	19,496
L. Kennard	18	43	17,165
1971/72			
F. T. Winter	31	72	62,863
W. A. Stephenson	45	113	55,542
T. F. Rimell	31	63	49,141
T. Forster	25	50	42,336
R. Turnell	23	46	37,215
F. Walwyn	30	59	36,847
G. Balding	29	56	32,149
D. Barons	40	86	31,113
H. Thomson Jones	19	41	28,020
K. Oliver	23	46	26,722
D. Gondolfo	22	36	26,412
R. Armytage	16	37	21,988

Comparisons as to whether Golden Miller, Cottage Rake or Arkle were the greatest Cheltenham Gold Cup winners are purely hypothetical and perhaps rather tedious. However, what can be said is that all three horses were multiple winners of the Gold Cup and great individuals. When comparisons are being made, one must compare like with like and when one discusses National Hunt racing, comparisons before the 1920's, when the Cheltenham Gold Cup and Champion Hurdle were instigated, and post 1930, are meaningless.

Since the 1920's Stewart Wight and Ken Oliver have by far the best record as public trainers in Scotland. Stewart Wight rode as an amateur from 1919 to 1926 and as a professional during the 1926/27 season. Among the best horses which he trained were Lord Joicey's Bramble Tudor, who won nineteen races, including the Great Yorkshire Chase in 1955 and Inversible, who won the Grand Sefton over the National course in 1937.

Stewart Wight won the Scottish Grand National twice with the Ken Oliver owned and ridden Sanvina in 1950 and Fincham in 1960. Probably his greatest training feat was in the 1954/55 season, when he won fifty-nine races, more than any other trainer in the British Isles. He was well known for teaching young men, both amateur and professional, and his protégés included Dick Curran, Mick Batchelor, Tommy Robson, Ken Oliver, Reg Tweedie, and Danny Moralee. He retired in 1960 because of ill-health, just when Ken was getting going as a public trainer.

As already stated at the beginning of this chapter, Ken had the highest regard for Stewart Wight, both as a trainer and as a friend. Ken says of him: "Much of our success must be down to what I learned from Stewart when I had horses with him. The help he gave us when we were training under permit and under licence at Hassendean Bank was invaluable".

Rhona also remembers Stewart with great affection: "I drove him to what I think was his last race meeting. He was a wonderful person and extremely popular with everyone in racing. Long before I married Ken, when I was still training under my father's permit, Stewart was very helpful to me".

Both Ken and Rhona are adamant that Stewart Wight was the greatest Scottish trainer ever and I (Rupert Collens) have quoted at some length what they have said about him. I know things are very different now to when Stewart was training so many winners, but in my opinion the Olivers' training record is as impressive if not more impressive than Stuart's.

Ken and Rhona have trained over 1000 winners including horses trained under permit. They have won five Scottish Grand Nationals, and Ken rode the winner of the same race in 1950, they have had six winners at the Cheltenham National Hunt Festival, won the Fred Withington twice and most of the important chases run on Northern courses such as Haydock, Hexham, Newcastle, Kelso and Perth. On the hurdling front, if Drumikill had jumped the last when he was second to Persian War, they would have won a Champion Hurdle and they did win both of the important hurdle races at Aintree, the Liverpool and Lancashire Hurdles.

In itself, Wyndburgh's record in the Grand National is remarkable, with three seconds and a fourth out of six attempts. The only other horse to compete in six Grand Nationals since the war was West Tip.

Ken and Rhona believe that Stewart Wight was Scotland's best National Hunt trainer, but with 1000 winners under their belt, the Olivers must come a very close second.

8

THE TEVIOTDALE FARMERS' CLUB

It is easy to forget that while Ken Oliver has achieved so much the family roots are very much in the soil. Indeed throughout his lifetime Ken has remained an active farmer. It has always been so in the Oliver family and while his forebears at one time farmed extensively in the Hawick district, Ken's domain is confined to Hassendean Bank and its 400 acres.

Though less involved now in the day-to-day activities which are largely shared between Rhona and grandson, Clive Forster, Ken still has his finger close to the pulse of the farming industry and nowhere is that heartbeat better appreciated than in the convivial and relaxed gatherings of the Teviotdale Farmers' Club at its regular winter meetings.

The Teviotdale Farmers' Club is an unique organisation. There is absolutely nothing remotely akin to it anywhere in the farming world and, even after 130 years, to be proposed and accepted for membership is still regarded as an honour. The history is typical of so much of the Oliver family in that it owes its existence to Ken's grandfather, James Oliver, applying to join a gentleman farmers' club in Hawick and being blackballed. Ken heard the story from his father: "Grandfather thought well, damn them, I'll start my own club." He did just that in 1859 and today that Farmers' Club has a membership of close to 150 farmers and others with a keen interest in agriculture. The rival club withered and died not long after James Oliver was rejected. Indeed the Teviotdale Farmers' Club is the second oldest such organisation after the Farmers' Club in Whitehall and its success over the years is in no small measure due to the Oiver family - all of the club secretaries have been Olivers.

Today the club meets on the second Thursday evening in the winter months from October to March in the Thornwood Hotel which, by a quirk of history, was originally built as a private residence by Ken's grandfather James. The format may seem a shade anachronistic to some, but those who have the best interests of the club at heart would never allow things to change. Members are expected to wear a suit. Dinner is served with the club president, the guest speaker, the joint secretaries and perhaps another guest seated at the top table. After dinner the Loyal Toast is proposed by the president who will then say: "Gentlemen you may now smoke." Woebetide anyone who lights up before then!

The guest speaker will then be invited to "give his paper to the club," and most certainly, not to lecture. At the conclusion of this "paper" the club president will go around the room addressing each member in turn by name: "Mr. Smith have you anything to say?" Mr. Smith may have little to add apart from thanking the speaker or he may have a serious question to which he will expect a considered reply, and so it goes on until every member has had his chance. It's a format which promotes discussion and is much envied because there is nothing worse for anyone chairing a meeting than those anxious few moments when he asks for the first question from the floor. Silence at that point can kill discussion - it never happens in this club.

The debate can be, and often is, vigorous but it will be unfailingly polite. For as long as most of the present membership can remember, Ken has had the last word and whatever he has said will always attract attention, if not total agreement. However, a further attraction of the Teviotdale Farmers' Club is that a complete record of every meeting held since its foundation in 1859 has been kept. The records are published periodically in book form as the *Transactions of the Teviotdale Farmers' Club*. These records are not just a commentary on the state of farming at any particular date, but rather an insight into the whole life of the community. The club in its early days had considerable political clout. This, after all, was in an age when there was no National Farmers Union, and its views were very often considered by the Minister of Agriculture of the time regarding the pressing issues of the age. For example, representations have been made over the years on the Agricultural Holdings Act, Game Laws, Foot and Mouth Disease, Agricultural Labourers Holiday Bill, railway and postal facilities and the dipping of sheep, to list but just a few.

Clearly these topics were of a very serious nature at the time, but looking back through the transactions today it is very often possible to raise a smile or two. Consider one issue which evidently was a matter of serious concern - "The Ravages of Mice on the Hill Farms of the District." According to Mr. Grieve of Skelfhill, "serious damage was being done to hill grazings, and a committee should be appointed to look into the matter and report back at an early date."

That committee was duly formed and subsequently inspected several farms where they found that: "The mice had steadily increased in numbers and in the extent of their devastation over the past five years. They had so thoroughly consumed the pasture which should be ready for the sheep in the spring months on the lower and more sheltered grounds, that these were now abandoned by them for the higher regions, where the work of destruction was still in active progress." Serious stuff, indeed, and obviously of great concern to sheep farmers. A lengthy report was prepared and the activities of the mice were widely reported in the local press. In fact it was reckoned that the mice had destroyed up to 30% of the natural grazing, but curiously these predators were apparently different from the usual field mice: "They were from three to four inches long, with a short stumpy tail, bright piercing eyes and large ears."

In a striking parallel to many of the ecological arguments of the present day, it was suggested that the mice had increased dramatically because gamekeepers had had been over zealous in controlling birds of prey and weasels which would naturally have kept numbers in check.

In 1891 the subject was raised yet again by Charles Scott of Milsington, whose grandson Charles was to prove such a top class amateur rider in the 1950's and 1960's riding many winners, including Merryman II in the Foxhunters' at Liverpool prior to stepping down in favour of Gerry Scott (no relation) who won the Scottish Grand National in 1959 and the Grand National itself the following year. Mr. Scott reported that the problem was still serious and yet again a committee was set up to investigate. This group had no doubt that the plague was due to the actions of the gamekeepers and accordingly "memorialised" the Duke of Buccleuch as the largest landowner in the district on the situation. There is no record of the ducal response.

Equally improbable as this plague to the modern age was the animated debate which took place both on the subject of holidays for farmworkers and whether shepherds should be paid a cash wage instead of merely being allowed to keep a small flock or "pack" of their own. The holiday question was one which provoked real fire in the spring of 1888. That acrimony related to a bill introduced into the House of Commons proposing that farmworkers should be entitled to no less than four days holiday in the year! The members of the club were "unanimous in condemning the plan," saying that instead of bringing benefits to the workers it "would do them a very great injury." One member went further: "To think that labourers would be benefitted by getting four days holiday in the year was simply nonsense," and he believed that "99% of farm servants would prefer the present system." That "present" system was one where the workers were allowed certain local fair days off work once certain tasks had been completed, but they were few and far between.

Foxhunting is a highly controversial issue in the late Twentieth Century, and so it seems to have been over 100 years ago in some quarters. One of the club's members, the Rev. John Thompson, gave a paper in which he was severely critical of the sport: "The Borderland has long been famous for many sports in the open air. There is leaping, wrestling, racing, cock-fighting, dog-fighting and pugilistic encounters. And in all these pastimes he would take the liberty of remarking that there was an element of fair play - one cock against another, one dog against another and so on. But in foxhunting the scene was changed "40 or 50 hounds against a single poor fox." The Rev. Thompson was also "amazed that ladies especially could let their names be recorded in the newspapers as being present at the death of a fox!" Needless to say Mr. Thompson's viewpoint came in for a good deal of criticism, for those were the days when virtually every farmer in the land followed hounds.

For Ken it is not just the fact that he and his family have been associated with the club which makes it such a special organisation: "The very fact that such details have been kept over the years is marvellous in itself, but it's the sheer amount of information which has been collected which I treasure. For example, we have records of the average prices for many classes of livestock sold in the district for well over 130 years. That is a valuable historical record and one with which I am very proud to have been involved."

Ken himself was admitted to the club in December 1933, just after he had joined his father in the family business. It was a time of adversity for the farming industry and low prices were testing the financial staying power of many long established family businesses. A measure of the decline in livestock prices can be seen from the club's records which show that in 1921 Cheviot lambs averaged 34/6 or £1.87½p, while by 1933 the same class of sheep had sunk to 14/9 (73p) per head. Across the whole spectrum of the farming scene it was more or less the same with product prices down by half on the period immediately after the First World War. Ken can recall still those dark days. "It really was desperate and some farms were just abandoned. Even as auctioneers dependent on commission, life was difficult."

Not surprisingly, this crisis engendered great political activity with the

Teviotdale Farmers' Club being foremost in pointing out to the Government the necessity for an effective and rapid remedy. Motions and submissions were made, and one result was the passing of the Agricultural Marketing Act which saw the establishment of the various milk marketing boards. The Minister of Agriculture at the time was Walter Elliot, and to this day his widow, Baroness Elliot of Harwood, is the only lady ever to be invited to address the club - and that only happened in the past few years. Baroness Elliot was conscious both of the honour and prestige of the club: "My late husband always used to take note of what your members said, and even today when I attend agricultural debates in the House of Lords consideration of the affairs of this club are a great help to me." That evening the Baroness was made an Honorary Life Member of the club.

From the early 1930's things improved steadily for most farmers through the Government paying various subsidies to help keep them in business and to ensure that they could compete with cheap imports from overseas. Indeed in 1935 a subsidy of 5/- (25p) per hundredweight (50kgs. liveweight) was paid on fat cattle - a fantastic rate considering that the total value of the beasts would be no more than £20. However, hill farmers fared less well than their counterparts on the lowlands from the necessity of providing food during the Second World War and at one meeting of the club, Midlothian farmer, W.I. Elliot of Middletown, was clearly steamed up about the whole thing: "We are merely voices in the wilderness as far as the Government is concerned." Mr. Elliot obviously did not like being told what farmers must do by the authorities, as indeed they were during wartime, and expressed total revulsion at the thought of golf courses being ploughed up: "Golfers will have to learn to lay their approaches from the nearest tattie bed."

The son of that particular member of the Elliot family - Douglas or W.I.D. Elliot, as he was often known, went on to become one of the best rugby players Scotland has ever produced and captained the team in the early 1950's. He was also an able sheep farmer - and a firm friend of Ken. Indeed the pair were involved in many escapades together.

That particular meeting of the club must have been one of the most acrimonious during the war with a great deal of moaning by many farmers. One who apparently lost his temper was Tom Douglas, a veritable terrier of man: "We ought to put up with low prices for as long as we can. The main thing is to win the war. It will be better to survive on overdrafts than to survive as slaves!" Indeed during the period of entire war one finds remarkably few references to the national situation and while one cannot doubt the patriotism of the farming community, it is sad to look back and see just how insular were some of the views then expressed.

Things changed with the advent of peace. A certain Major Kenneth Oliver is recorded as speaking out in December 1945: "We might say that the time is coming when the masses in the country are going to say that the land is their heritage, and that farmers should be paid a salary by the Government for looking after it. You may say that such a view is taking matters too far, but we have to discuss the possibility because a lot of people are thinking that way." Ken's politics have always favoured the path of free enterprise and on another occasion he, in a light-hearted manner, put down one of the club's stalwarts, John Tullie, who had suggested that the Government should be approached with a view to acquiring redundant Nissen huts for housing cattle: "Let's make farming profitable by all means, but don't fly away to the Government for farm steadings. Mr Tullie would then become No.99 State Servant in his farm at Bownhill, instead of a self-respecting farmer!"

This too was the age when enormous scientific advances were made in agriculture and one of the best attended meetings "for very many years" occurred when Dr. Stephen Watson - later one of Britain's foremost agricultural scientists - gave a paper on the benefits of lime and fertiliser to crops. It may seem odd to the present day generation of farmers, but less than fifty years ago much of practical farming was based on trial and error and past experiences. Dr. Watson put the farmers of Teviotdale on the right track.

It was an age also when the whole of Europe was teetering on the verge of starvation. Indeed many medical specialists reckoned that the diet of the average Briton was poorer in the aftermath of war than actually during it. It was therefore a time when farmers were encouraged by a whole means of grants and subsidies to produce as much as they could in the certainty that there would be a guaranteed price for everything. It was, in short, a time of farming prosperity and expansion, but needless to say farmers in general did not like the rules and regulations which went with all the new schemes and those in Teviotdale seemed to spend hours arguing over each new initiative. There is no indication, however, that they were unwilling to take the Government's cash. Some of that money was invested in new devices such as tractors and combine harvesters, although from the records it appears that a few of the old hands were less than convinced that these machines "would last," and it would be a wise farmer who still kept a few Clydesdale horses.

One essential annual ingredient in the dealings of the club is a review of the previous year's farming by the president. As Ken says: "Each of the very many presidents I have known - they hold office for a two-year period - has had his own style, but when one looks back and re-reads the reviews it is amazing how the memory is jogged." Among the more sobering reviews was that given at the end of 1947 by Robert Grieve of Southfield, Hawick. Robert was the third generation of his family to have been a member and indeed his family were tenants of the Duke of Buccleuch for over 200 years. 1947 must have been one of the worst years in his and many other families' experience.

"In the third week of January winter set in and never altered until March 16th. Storm followed storm and things went from bad to worse. Hay started to run out on many farms. Disaster followed disaster, and farmers were down in the very depths. Hay had to be dropped by aeroplane - something quite unheard of before. On the hills there were severe losses and the bad lambing weather in April made it the worst year for many sheep farmers in living memory, and long before it."

Officially there was an decrease of over 900,000 lambs born in Scotland that year. Strangely enough, that atrocious winter was followed by one of the best summers on record. But for the country as a whole, affairs were at an extremely low ebb. Foreign exchange was all but exhausted and even potatoes were rationed, but said Mr. Grieve: "Perhaps now the nation will realise just how much it needs farmers."

Over the years Ken assisted his father in the general running of the club, and readily admits: "Most of the really hard work and administration was done by the staff in the mart office." Farmers are notoriously slow to part with cash, but when it came to the collection of subscriptions that was not so difficult: "We did it quite painlessly. You see most of the members were customers of ours at the mart so at the end of the year we just knocked their subscription off a cheque or added it to a bill. Our accounts were always in good order." Ken finally succeeded his father as secretary of the club in 1953 - a position he holds to this day with his son Stuart as joint secretary.

Just occasionally the debates and discussions, not to say all-out arguments, would turn to bloodstock and on at least one occasion Ken's great friend Alistair Paton spoke: "There is no reason why horse breeding, already practised by many farmers as a hobby, should not become an industry. The ideal mare is one of a thoroughbred type - of good conformation, bone, strength and correct outlook - but above all free from any taint of hereditary disease."

He was also quick to counter those who criticised the showground:

"Prizes and medals at shows indicate a freedom from hereditary disease and the ability to move - and that goes for all classes of livestock." But his wisest words came when he said: "There is no doubt that we in this area can breed good horses - The Callant and Wyndburgh stand out head and shoulders above the rest." However, there was also a word of warning for some: "It is no use expecting that you can treat a mare and her pony as you would by putting a ewe and her lamb on to the hill. You must have an interest in and understanding of horses, but to keep them is neither very difficult or expensive."

Towards the end of the 1950's farming came under increasing attack from many sides because of the high level of subsidies, but Ken was quick to defend his friends: "Farmers have had some quite good years recently but expenses are high and if it were not for the assistance given by the Government then they might as well give up altogether." He was also to the fore in organising an evening in 1959 when his old friend Senator John D. Sheridan would address the club and it proved to be a great success. The Senator, in racy form, put forward his philosophy for life: "A man should live as if he would die tomorrow, but farm as if he was going to live forever." He also tabulated some of the changes he had witnessed in his years of exporting cattle from Eire to Scotland: "I've seen a 1,000 head of cattle in Kelso each Friday with business conducted in the local hostelries late on in the day to the extent that by the time the deals were struck no-one was in a position to care much about anything. That is all gone now - and perhaps, more's the pity."

Perhaps the greatest evening in the long and distinguished history of the Teviotdale Farmers' Club came on November 20th, 1959, when the centenary dinner was held in the Tower Hotel in Hawick - the regular venue for all meetings until its closure ten years ago. On that occasion the great, the noble and the good joined company with the farmers of Teviotdale in an evening of great celebration. Chairing the occasion was Billy Kirkpatrick of Chapelhill who, besides being a farmer, also acted as a part-time secretary for the National Farmers Union.

Billy stood no nonsense and he decreed that it should not be an evening for "stuffed shirts." The local newspaper, The Hawick News, commented thus: "Lounge suits had been prominently marked on all the tickets so that even at the top table tweeds and homespuns were the order of the evening, making for a degree of homeliness and universal equality that always seems to mark Border farmers' gatherings."

The toast list was extensive with the Duke of Buccleuch paying tribute to the club and its many activities while Lord Netherorpe, who as plain

Jim Turner had been president of the NFU of England and Wales, soon threw away his notes in expounding the future role of agriculture. Meanwhile Ken's old friend, George Hedley proposed the toast to the guests while he himself, for once, brought up the rear in replying to a tribute to his secretarial skills. Years later he still remembers it all lucidly: "It was one of those evenings in life that can never be forgotten. There we had them all, dukes and lords, sitting down with the working farmers of the district and getting on famously. That really is what life is about. We are all in this together an we have to pull together."

Since then the Teviotdale Farmers' Club has continued to thrive with as great a variety of speakers and topics as ever. Some have failed occasionally to hold the total attention of the secretary. One such was the banker who went on at some length during an evening which followed a major sale in the mart where Ken, after performing his duties in the rostrum, had adjourned to the bar. It was too much to expect that his attention could be held by facts and figures and he duly nodded off. However, after close on an hour he suddenly came to, looked around him, then remarked in a voice that everyone could hear: "Good God is that boring bastard still blithering on?" Needless to say the boring banker soon sat down to the great relief of the company. Perhaps that is what club secretaries are appointed for!

Even to this day Ken will not miss a meeting if he can help it, and only earlier this year the author (Dan Buglass) joined him at Hassendean Bank after a day at Carlisle races to go to the club. Ken's racing days are never quiet or dry, but he was still going stronger than anyone else well past midnight.

Away from the Teviotdale Farmers' Club Ken was, for many years, associated with Herd's Supper - a social evening for shepherds and farmworkers - in a hall in Hawick. As ever his organisational skills in association with that never failing love of a good party ensured that these nights were a huge success. "I remember one in particular, we must have had about 200 at it, so that it was almost like two parties at either end of the hall. Well, late on when the formal part was over and it came time to tidy up, we discovered about half-a-dozen out for the count. We just loaded them up into a van, dumped them in a cattle pen at the mart, and left them to sober up!"

As a farmer Ken has always been recognised as being one who could grow excellent crops and produce top class livestock. For that, considering how little time he used to spend at home, he was dependent on a reliable staff, and he has never forgotten them: "Over the years we've been very lucky and people have stayed with us for years. Bill Hughes was in charge for a very long time, and he knew what to do without ever being told. Bill and his wife Ellen were almost like part of the family and they were never afraid to help in the house with organising a party - or clearing up afterwards." Those parties are another story.

1970. Mr. Rimmer leading in The Spaniard after winning the Scottish Grand National at Ayr.

1971. Even Keel winning the Express Chase at Sandown.

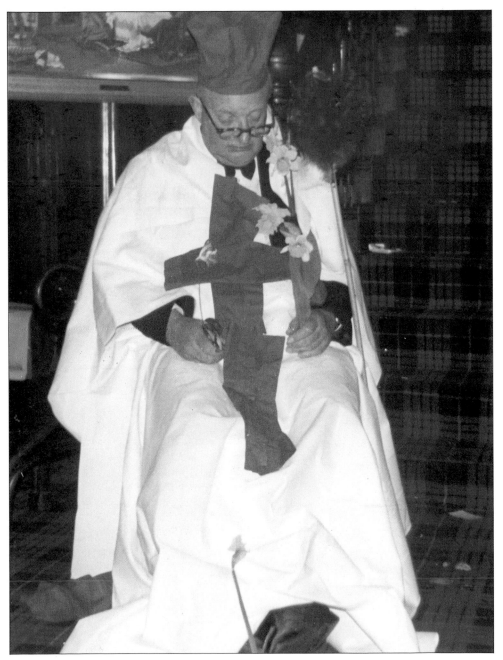

'The Benign Bishop'.

1972. Young Ashleaf and Tommy Stack on the way to victory in the Greenall Whitley at Haydock.

1972. Stuart (nearest to camera) on the way to be third in a hurdle at Cheltenham on The Benign Bishop.

1973. Ron Barry canters to the start on Earls Castle, owned by Her Majesty Queen Elizabeth The Queen Mother, before winning at Ayr.

1979. Mrs. L. Carr leads in Fighting Fit, the winner of the Ayr Scottish Grand National ridden by Chris Hawkins.

c. 1972. Rhona and the hard-pulling Even Keel on the gallops.

9

DONCASTER BLOODSTOCK SALES

To make his life as complicated and busy as possible must seem to many observers as being the Ken Oliver motto in life. Not content with being a livestock auctioneer, estate agent, farmer and racehorse trainer - and considerably successful in all of these fields - in the early 1960's Ken set out to become involved in the selling of high class bloodstock by resurrecting the defunct Doncaster Sales. As ever, when Ken sets out to accomplish anything, it was done with style and determination. More than thirty years later that venture has no need to question its achievements. The name of Doncaster Bloodstock Sales Limited is renowned throughout the British Isles and beyond and forever associated with its twin founders - Ken Oliver and Willie Stephenson.

Ken's association with Willie Stephenson dates back to the days when he rode Choir Belle for him and over the years they became the firmest of friends, frequently indulging their outrageous sense of fun at race meetings all over the country. Despite this, at heart they were both hard-headed businessmen who could spot a niche in the market and capitalise on the potential.

So how did Doncaster Bloodstock Sales Limited get off the ground? As always with Ken and Willie it had to be unconventional: "I had asked Willie up to the Kelso Horse Sales and after Rhona and I had been at Perth races we stopped in at the Buccleuch Arms Hotel in St. Boswells to meet him. As soon as I got in Willie jumped off his seat at the bar, grabbed hold of me and took me into a private room of the proprietor, Donald Wares."

There was no beating about the bush on the part of Willie Stephenson: "You and I, Ken, are going to re-start the Doncaster sales. Tattersalls sales at Newmarket are not very popular with a lot of people and I think we can make a go of it. The other lot need some competition." Ken's response was swift: "Right, if you're that keen then I'm game, let's have a right go at this." The rest is history with a whole host of leading performers both over jumps and on the flat having been purchased at Doncaster.

Obviously some basic organisation was necessary and most of that fell to Ken: "We planned to hold the very first sale in a marquee, but shortly before the sale I 'phoned Willie to find out what we were going to do about putting some money into the business. Willie sent me a cheque for £150 and I lodged a similar amount in the Royal Bank of Scotland in Hawick - and that's all the capital we ever put into Doncaster Bloodstock Sales. So far the peak turnover has been over £17 million, but with the recent changes in VAT making such a positive difference, I can see that total being exceeded in the not too distant future."

Now of course, a wide variety of sales are held at Doncaster but an early innovation was to stage yearling sales during the week of the oldest of all the Classics - the St. Leger - in 1963, just one full year after the company was established. In those early days gaining support from both breeders and trainers was essential, and that was where Ken's marvellous skills in persuading even the most reluctant consignors to send horses to him came into play: "I thought we had better go to Ireland because in the old days the Irish were great supporters of Doncaster. I especially courted that wonderful lady breeder, Peg Watt, and spent a great deal of time trying to get her to send us some yearlings. She wouldn't make a decision there and then, but it was agreed that I should phone her a few days later at noon."

An anxious few days followed because Ken knew that if he could get Peg Watt's yearlings the interest would be enormous. The appointed hour arrived, and by chance it just happened to be on the first day of the Cheltenham Festival in March: "I was sweating like hell, wondering what she was going to say, but when she said we were to get her yearlings I knew we had made a major breakthrough."

Peg Watt was to become a firm friend and some years later, after Ken had sold one of her yearlings for a "bloody good price," a party ensued in the bar: "Ken, my man," said Peg, "You've got the grandest voice. I think you must have been suckled on port!" Not many auctioneers have heard their praises extolled in quite such a liquid form.

Ken's friend Padge Berry was another to support him and he was quoted when he first chose to send horses to Doncaster: "I prefer to sell at home. In fact the only auctions I sell at are at Doncaster. When Ken and Willie

130

Stephenson re-started the sales, Ken asked me to help him out by sending over a few three-year-olds. Ken, I said, you've been such a tremendous help to me that I'll do anything to assist you." That help has never, or ever, will be forgotten.

Prices initially were modest, but trade developed: "God, I nearly fell out of the rostrum when I sold one for 5000 guineas, but we concentrated very much on the National Hunt angle and it's just grown and grown from that very first sale when we catalogued about 200 head." Staffing was largely in the hands of the office personnel from the mart at Hawick under the capable charge of head cashier, Jack McCulloch. The staff from Hawick enjoyed their trips to Doncaster and not a few parties were held when all the hard work was completed. To this day, despite the vast expansion of Doncaster Bloodstock Sales Limited, the company is still based in the Borders in Hawick: "It's a good place to live and work, and we've never felt under any pressure to move."

Ken and Rhona were chiefly responsible for the specialist work of gathering pedigree information and arranging the sales catalogues, but it soon started to become too much: "Things went better than we ever anticipated, and we soon found ourselves working half the night with the dining room table at Hassendean Bank absolutely covered in paper. It was verging on the chaotic." Indeed it was, and even with Ken's old friend of so many years, Alan Innes, who had a marvellous knowledge of thoroughbred pedigrees, helping out, disaster was never far away: "One night after Alan had been here he took a great wad of entries home with him. He stopped near his farm of Windywalls in the midst of a snowstorm and opened the car door. Well, the wind got in and next thing there were bits of paper flying all over the Borders and over at least half the Buccleuch hunting country!"

The time had obviously come to take on extra and specialist staff which was something Willie Stephenson had been thinking about for some time: "Willie said that he had approached Jack Botterill who at the time was the up-and-coming man at the Ascot Sales." The response from this most able and gifted auctioneer was disparaging to say the least with his opinion running along the lines that Doncaster would never work and that Willie and Ken were wasting their time, not to say their money.

Second thoughts were urgently required, but once again Willie came up with a suggestion worth investigating: "He said, come to Newbury - I think I've got just the man we need." That man turned out to be Harry Beeby who, in the intervening years, has become one of the most respected figures in the bloodstock industry with an incredible knowledge of pedigrees,

131

form and people." Harry was at the time working for a firm in London, but he had a long connection with the bloodstock industry through his father George who trained two Cheltenham Gold Cup winners as well a whole host of other jumping winners.

Harry Beeby is among the most polite and charming of men and on that initial meeting he made some impression: "I always remember it, and I still pull his leg about when we were first introduced. Harry must have lifted his hat to me at least ten times." The pair hit it off at once: "I took to Harry straight away, and he joined us and has made a great success of the business ever since. We would never have made the progress we have without Harry Beeby."

Harry Beeby's own recollections of that meeting with Ken and Willie are revealing: "It was the Schweppes Gold Cup at Newbury, and of course I had heard bits and pieces about Ken. Meeting him, however, was something different. He and Willie were very similar - both in a state of perpetual motion."

Arrangements were made for Harry and his wife to come north on the sleeper to Hawick to have further discussions: "We came up in horrible weather and arrived at ten-to-six in the morning, allegedly to go point-to-pointing, but that was cancelled, so we spent the time discussing the possibility of my working with Ken. Before it was time for us to go back on the night train - Ken was as ever in a hurry to get off to Ireland to see Padge Berry - I was virtually a member of the staff of Doncaster Bloodstock Sales." There have never been any regrets: "At the time I had not the slightest intention of moving to Scotland, but it has turned out to be the best thing that ever happened." As to working with Ken: "He's always been marvellously supportive. He gave me my head at a very early stage, which I suppose he had to, since he was involved in so many different things at the time, but I can honestly say that we got on famously right from the very start."

Initially Harry frequently stayed with Ken and Rhona at Hassendean Bank, and just occasionally, as Ken recounts with a decidedly wicked grin, the slumbers of the just were liable to be disturbed in no uncertain fashion: "I love my garden and everything that grows in it, and I will not put up with rabbits spoiling all the hard work. That was the situation one summer, but I had my eye on the little buggers and was determined to have them."

The plans were laid: "One morning I got up early, at about five. The best room for spotting them was the guest room where Harry was sleeping. I saw a couple, let fly with the gun and bagged a brace. Harry was more than surprised but at least I woke him up!"

Next to join the company was yet another character of the bloodstock scene, Michael "Mouse" White who teamed up with Harry Beeby in 1966. Ken remembers how a certain well-known figure on the northern racing scene approached him in near desperation: "Charlie Hall came to me one evening at the bar in Punches Hotel in Doncaster and asked if I had a job that would suit his nephew. The boy apparently spent all his time with Sam Hall and was driving the family round the bend, while his brother was playing it safe in the family solicitor's business. Clearly this lad was not interested in things like that. The only thing that seemed to get him going was horses. It was quite obvious that the entire Hall family were at a total loss as to what they should do with young Michael White." Ken did not take long to hire this young colt.

Mouse certainly found his niche - "He's a great judge of a horse." That judgement is now well recognised and he can quote pedigrees and form backwards, forwards and sideways, such is his expertise. His tips in the Fox and Hounds, the local pub in Denholm, are always keenly sought after, though to play dominoes with him is to invite disaster. He always seems to win.

Mouse and Ken have always worked well together, and one particular skill which Mouse possesses has worked advantageously for the firm, according to Ken: "He's an excellent race-reader and I was delighted when he started to do racecourse commentaries all over the north of England and in Scotland. It's a valuable connection, but I regret that he doesn't get as much opportunity now since the advent of SIS on most courses, but undoubtedly he's got a knowledge that many of the commentators do not have." In turn Mouse simply says of his mentor: "He's become a legend in his own lifetime, and very few people achieve that."

Harry and Mouse, under the guidance of Ken and Willie Stephenson, rapidly developed the whole business to the extent that they were soon joined by Michael Dale of whom Ken says: "He is a great man to have behind the scenes. Michael does a lot of the background work that's an essential part of the operation." In more recent times another face joined the force: "A star was born when young Henry Beeby followed his father. I have the greatest respect for Henry. He really knows his horses and gets on well with everyone. He's a first rate auctioneer, but what I really like about Henry is that he takes time to ask advice from Rhona and me, and I find that very touching from a young man. Henry has so much talent, he could go right to the top anywhere." When Henry became the father of a young son, Ken was quick to say: "I'm so pleased that the family connection will

133

be carried on - in fact I've arranged that the youngest Beeby and I should sell ten lots each at Doncaster in twenty years time!"

Henry's greatest coup to date is one in which Ken takes great pride: "All our auctioneering staff go round the country a great deal inspecting yearlings before they are accepted for our big sales and so it was that Henry went to visit Pam Sly's stud near Northhampton to see this particular yearling filly." Henry was mighty impressed by this yearling, but her breeder thought she was "much too small to be any good." Henry persisted and eventually the filly was entered and later sold.

That diminutive filly rejoiced in the name of Lyric Fantasy, and since she has been described as the "wonder sprinter" or the "pocket rocket" as she ran away with many of the top prizes in the 1992 flat season, including the Queen Mary Stakes at Royal Ascot, the Nunthorpe Stakes at York and the Sales Super Sprint at Newbury, clocking up winnings of almost £200,000 in the process for her trainer Richard Hannon. Lyric Fantasy was purchased at Doncaster for a relatively modest 12,500 guineas by Richard Hannon on behalf of the Queen's racing manager, Lord Carnarvon, and her success helped the trainer to a staggering 154 winners in the full season with gross winnings of over £1.7 million.

In the autumn Lyric Fantasy again changed hands for 340,000 guineas at Newmarket when she was sold to John Magnier of the world-famous, Coolmore Stud in Ireland. She remained, however, with Richard Hannon, who over the years has made a speciality of buying sensibly priced yearlings at Doncaster. Interestingly, Henry Beeby's assessment of Lyric Fantasy's apparently pony-sized stature being irrelevant has proved to be correct. During the winter months Richard Hannon reported that she has grown by at least a couple of inches.

Testimony as to the quality of horses bought and sold at Doncaster was never more in evidence than at the 1993 Cheltenham Festival. No less than seven winners over the three days of superlative racing had previously passed through the Doncaster ring - Deep Sensation, Travado, Young Hustler, Ushers Island, Gaelstrom, Thumbs Up and Second Schedual. Ken retired from active auctioneering once Harry Beeby and his team were firmly installed. One notable incident is still fresh, however: "I had been selling and knocked this horse down to a buyer on the far side and didn't realise that the microphone was still switched on. So when the clerk asked me who had got the horse I turned and said - the fellow over there with a face like an ape! I think he must have been quite a decent chap, because I didn't get sued and he paid up."

On another famous occasion in the early days Ken was selling while his partner, Willie Stephenson, stood beside him watching the proceedings. Suddenly, as Ken was about to take a bid from a woman on the other side of the ring, the entire gathering heard Willie shout: "D-don't t-take her b-bid - she's pissed!" The woman in question just happened to be Willie's wife, Bobbie!

Similarly, the work involved in drawing up the sale catalogues is quite enormous and mistakes can occasionally be made. In one instance a certain horse was described as being "big and awkward" instead of "backward." The upshot was that the horse in question sold well above expectations because everyone noticed the printing error and paid particular attention

Over the years the facilities at Doncaster have been vastly improved with superb accommodation and amenities, but Ken was always one for a little bit of psychology: "Right from the start I told Willie Stephenson that where there's an auction ring you must also have a bar very close at hand. We made sure of that damned soon after we began."

National Hunt bloodstock remains the core of the Doncaster business and over the years the sales have been supported by most of the leading trainers as well as those with smaller yards looking for bargains. Ken has seen them all and most of them are firm friends: "David Nicholson, Josh Gifford and Nicky Henderson are all regulars as indeed is Martin Pipe." Ken has the highest regard for Martin Pipe who has single-handedly re-written the record books: "Martin knows his horses and is a wonderful trainer. What I find particularly interesting is that many other trainers are now following Martin's methods, including Ian Balding who trained the great Mill Reef and many winners for the Queen."

Martin and Ken met up at Ayr at the Scottish Grand National meeting in April 1993 where the champion trainer took the richest race in Scottish jumping with his top weighted, Run for Free, not surprisingly, in view of Ken's great record in the race over the years, the two were soon talking horses and racing - indeed what else? An adjournment to the bar was deemed to be in order and there Martin's quick wit was soon to the fore: "You know Ken, I'm having the most hellish job deciding which jockey will ride for me after Peter Scudamore's retirement. I've been looking up your past form, and you weren't too bad yourself. I've got you on the short list."

Also on hand at Ayr on the same day was a rather more youthful jockey, Declan Murphy, who has ridden Deep Sensation to many of his wins and though only meeting the young Irishman for the first time Ken was much impressed: "He's a super chap who is so obviously a real horseman." The pair were soon immersed in conversation, with jockey and breeder clearly sharing a common enthusiasm but then Ken added: " I know that you come from a place in Limerick called Hospital, well that's where I have my tailor - a gentleman called Mr. Frazier. He's a grand fellow who looks after Padge Berry and me as well as our old friend and great Doncaster supporter, Peg Watt. And you know what Mr. Frazier said about dear old Peg? Well, he said - she's got the biggest arse I've ever measured!" Whether Ken is familiar with the exact scope of the lady's hindquarters is unknown, but he is certain about one thing: "She's got a very healthy bank balance, and that's because she always gets on so well selling at Doncaster."

Ken still visits Ireland on a regular basis, but certainly not as frequently as in the past: "I never seemed to be away from the country what with looking at yearlings and visiting Padge. However, when we were looking at horses I often had the assistance of my dear friend Jim Doherty." Friends they were, but there was a minor problem: "Old Jim had a most tremendously strong Cork accent, and I could never understand a bloody word he said. However, our last port of call invariably involved a refreshment and after a drink or two I could understand Jim fine. It's amazing what happens when the cork is out!"

Sadly Jim passed on, but even in death humour persisted: "His wife couldn't understand why he hadn't come down for breakfast one morning and sent his daughter up to investigate. She was soon downstairs with the simple pronouncement - 'mother, he's as dead as mutton!' By chance Ken was selling at Doncaster at the time: "We heard that poor Jim was dead very quickly, and everyone was very sad for he was one of the real characters."

Happily Jim's son Tom is still to the fore and has had some great prices for yearlings. However, on one occasion Tom had a yearling which was unsold. But outwith the ring a deal was done and that marvellously astute operator Jack Berry took the horse home after a little persuasion from Ken. That transaction started a lasting connection and in 1988 Jack Berry trained So Careful for Tom Doherty to win the Ayr Gold Cup at the most rewarding odds of 33-1.

Jack Berry is another of the current trainers who Ken admires: "He started at Doncaster in a small way buying cheap horses over the years and now hardly ever misses a sale. He is an absolute master at buying what may look like moderate yearlings and turning them out to win as two-year-olds. That's what training is all about - knowing your horses, doing them well and finding the right races for them. Jack Berry can certainly do that - and besides that he's such a grand man to do business with."

Ken and Jack Berry have been friends for many years and occasionally have held joint interests in horses together. One of the more recent of those partnerships, involved Ken and Jack's wife, Jo: "We shared this yearling by Swing Easy, and the most natural thing in the world seemed to be to call him Down the Middle. I couldn't manage to travel to see his début run but I did watch on television. He came out of the stalls and swung violently to the left, prompting the commentator to say - Down the Middle is going down anything but the middle!"

Next time out was at Carlisle and Ken and Rhona were there this time: "I asked Jack what our chances were, and he said - I've castrated your one and I'd like to castrate him again, I think I'll win the race but with the other horse I've got in the field." This was not the news that Ken had hoped for and he duly advised his friends of Jack's opinion. However, there are no certainties in racing and Down the Middle won very easily, though without carrying wagers on the part of the owners! Further fun was had with Down the Middle but he showed no inclination to jump hurdles and was eventually sold.

Both Ken and Willie Stephenson recognised from the very start of the Doncaster Sales that Ireland and a sound Irish connection would be vital in securing the long term future of their venture as many good National Hunt horses are bred in Ireland. They therefore decided that they must have Irish representation on the board of directors. Their first choice was inspired: "We were extremely lucky in getting Jack White, who is one of the most popular men in Ireland and one of the best judges of a horse you could ever wish to meet. It also helped that he is a qualified vet and there is no doubt that he was instrumental in getting business for us."

Sadly, for the last few years, Jack White has been in poor health and his brother-in-law, Jack Powell joined the Doncaster team with his great connections in the south-west of Ireland.

Timmy Hyde completes the Irish end of the team with his international reputation - "bred like a true thoroughbred," according to Ken. Among the other directors is Alan Mactaggart, who farms within a few miles of Ken: "Alan has been a friend for many years and he really knows his horses. It's all very well to tell other people what to do, but if they know you can actually do it yourself then there is so much more respect." Alan Mactaggart can certainly do it. He rode the great Freddie in his early races and won many point-to-points on his own horses as well as having frequent wins for other owners. In turn his sons David and Jeremy are

137

accomplished riders, but Alan's greatest thrill in recent times has come from watching the success of a horse he bred - Docklands Express. This horse, trained by Kim Bailey, has apparently unlimited courage.

A most welcome addition to the board of directors has been Liz Butcher, Willie Stephenson's daughter, who runs the highly successful saddler's business of Gibsons in Newmarket. But to be truly successful these days bloodstock auctioneers have to be international in their out-look, a trend which was seen many years ago by Ken and his colleagues: "You've got to be out there in the market and we've got at good team. In France we have Jack Dobbin based at Chantilly. Jack has brought us a lot of business over the years and my own friendship with him goes back to the time when I used to run the occasional horse at Auteil as he was always so helpful."

As ever with Ken there is a very fine line between business and plea-sure and some years ago one day at Doncaster Jack Dobbin introduced him to the King of Morrocco's brother-in-law who just happened to be a very keen golfer. The upshot was that both Jack and Ken were invited out as his guests to play golf at Rabat and Marrakesh. It was an experience not to be forgotten: "Unfortunately the King himself could not play with us as planned, but we were treated like royalty. We travelled around in huge limousines and stayed at the best hotel in Marrakesh the place where Winston Churchill used to go on holiday."

In more recent times an Italian agent, Giorgio Barsotti, has been appointed and Ken is very hopeful that the thriving racing industry in Italy will increasingly see Doncaster as a source of yearlings. Giorgio him-self is in no doubt: "We can get value for money at Doncaster and very nice people, who could ask for more?" But having all the agents in the world counts for nothing unless the basic team on the ground are up to the mark and certainly at Doncaster there have never been any reserva-tions on Ken's part: "The yard staff have to be right and we were lucky in the early days to have Tony Weir who was the racecourse yard manager and now, he has retired, we have Frank Groves. Both have been really helpful and it was great that Frank was given an award by the Thoroughbred Breeders Association."

One of the greatest days in the history of Doncaster Bloodstock Sales in recent times did not even occur within the confines of the ring at Doncaster, but rather some miles further north near Bishops Auckland in Co. Durham where the company were instructed to disperse the entire bloodstock interests of the late Arthur Stephenson. This proved a mighty undertaking but one which Ken and his team were more than proud to execute: "Arthur was an amazing man with a great knowledge of horses and among the very best of trainers. I consider it a great honour that we should have been asked to sell his horses."

The record of Arthur Stephenson as a trainer will seldom be equalled, far less eclipsed. Over a forty year period he trained no less than 2,632 winners including such great horses as Blazing Walker, Celtic Gold, Credit Call, Durham Edition, Kinmot Wullie and so many more. However, his greatest achievement was winning the 1987 Cheltenham Gold Cup with The Thinker. Always a quiet and modest man, Arthur was not even at Cheltenham, but rather at Hexham turning out an altogether more modest winner. "It was absolutely typical of Arthur to avoid Cheltenham,"says Ken: "He didn't like any kind of fuss, but he knew his horses as well as anyone I have ever known."

It was often said of Arthur Stephenson that he bought horses in the way that some farmers buy batches of cattle and he certainly much preferred to buy privately. However, there was nothing private about the dispersal of his entire string. Each and every horse was sold without reserve, but in truth there was no need for any reserve. Friends, spectators and buyers from all over the country thronged the ringside set up in a large farm building to witness history in the making.

When after seven hours Mouse White finally sold the last of the 127 horses the aggregate for the day stood at a staggering 1,159,000 guineas. After the sale Harry Beeby commented: "There hasn't been an event like it for years, and you probably won't ever see another one like it." Ken commented: "I think Arthur would have been pleased with the trade, but he wouldn't have said much" On a more serious note, however: "It's made me very proud to see how that small business which Willie Stephenson - Arthur's cousin - and I started all those years ago has grown and become such an integral part of the racing industry. I don't think we ever thought it would come to this, but like most things in life it's down to hard work and a good team. I just let them get on with things these days - most of the time".

The full range of fixtures held by Doncaster Bloodstock Sales Limited throughout the year is formidable. It starts with a one day sale in January which features a stallion show. Come March it's time for the famous "Breeze-Up" sales for two-year-olds in training, followed in turn by the "Lincoln Sales." May is one of the busiest months with a four-day event largely devoted to top class National Hunt horses. Sales are held in June and August but the St. Leger yearling sales in September are the main event of the summer. These in turn are followed by others in October and

November. Ken is justly proud of the company of which he remains vice-chairman: "I'm amazed really, especially when you remember that it all started at a party with Willie Stephenson and me putting in £150 each!"

It is natural for Ken to be proud of his achievements with Doncaster Bloodstock Sales, but it is interesting to hear what others have to say right across the spectrum of the bloodstock industry. Robert Sangster, Arabs apart, is one of the most influential owners worldwide: "I always like to attend Doncaster and buy a couple of early two-year-old types and have been delighted with my purchases over the years. These sales have a very friendly atmosphere." Jack Berry, who is renowned for getting value for money and turning out a whole string of two-year-old winners says: "Without a doubt my favourite place to buy - I wouldn't miss it." Richard Hannon, who of course made so much of Lyric Fantasy, is equally supportive: "A good, honest sale where I have bought some of my best winners."

National Hunt trainers are also keen supporters. Martin Pipe commented: "I find the spring sales are the complete National Hunt Sales with stores right through to horses with form." Meanwhile Nicky Henderson says: "I simply cannot afford to stay away from Doncaster." Ken himself is another one who will not miss a sale at Doncaster: "I just love it, especially meeting so many friends."

10

GARDENING AND GOLF

Rest has never been part of the Ken Oliver philosophy of life but recreation most certainly has. Indeed, Ken could almost claim that recreation has filled his life: "I've never regarded what I've done as being work. I've enjoyed practically everything I've ever done, and that makes me a very lucky person." However, in the true sense of the terminology, playing golf and a passion for gardening have come as near to recreation as anything.

The garden at Hassendean Bank bears ample testimony to a life-long interest in all things horticultural but golf and its intricacies is another matter: "I used to play a bit of golf when I was at school, but I was never any bloody good at it. As any golfer will tell you, it's a hellishly frustrating game unless it's played well." Determined that he should become an accomplished golfer, Ken went down to visit an uncle at Frinton in Essex: "Uncle was secretary of the local golf club and he introduced me to this amazing professional called Tingy, and it was from him that I learned anything I now know about playing golf."

Tingy's tutorial skills were keenly sought after in those days of the early 1930's: "He was among the best teachers of the game at the time and indeed he taught both the Duke of Windsor - later to become King Edward VII - and the Aga Khan, so you see I couldn't have had anyone better." After those sessions with Tingy, Ken was well and truly smitten with the golf bug and to this day he still manages a few holes before breakfast most summer mornings on the beautiful course at Minto, just a mile up the road from Hassendean Bank.

Ken's passion for the game is by no means confined to Minto: "Just after the war in the late 1940's I was riding quite a few winners for a gentleman by the name of Alex Mitchell, who really was a wonderful owner

141

to ride for and a person who was always so pleased when his horses won." Alex Mitchell was also a very keen golfer and a member of one of the most exclusive clubs in the world - the Honourable Company of Edinburgh Golfers who play at Muirfield on the East Lothian coast. This led to further developments in Ken's golfing experiences: "He was going to give me a racing saddle as a present for riding a winner." However, while I appreciated this kind offer I said to Alex: "It really is very kind of you, but father has provided me with all the necessary saddles." The gracious owner was not to be confounded: "I understand of course, but is there anything that I can do for you?"

Ken's reply was not long in coming: "Sir, is there any chance at all of you being able to get me accepted for membership at Muirfield? I would really love that." Alex Mitchell wasted no time and in a matter of a few weeks Ken joined the ranks of the Muirfield members who have always included many of the leading figures in Scottish life: "It's almost fifty years since I first became a member and it's undoubtedly been one of the great privileges of my life to play on the course and to meet so many nice people."

Half a century ago acceptance for membership was a rare honour and the waiting list considerable, but that is nothing compared to the present when applicants may have to wait for many years. Even being on the waiting list is no guarantee of eventual membership with such notable celebrities as Ludovic Kennedy and several leading figures in the Edinburgh legal establishment. To be a member at Muirfield is truly something, but for a guest of a member the welcome is fulsome and the hospitality is always immense.

Over the years Ken has played many rounds at Muirfield but there is one day he recalls with particular relish: "I went through to stay near Muirfield with my friends the Robertson-Durhams for a week to play golf. One day when I arrived to tee off I was introduced to the current South African amateur champion who was looking for a game." It proved to be quite a game with the South African being a contemporary of the great Bobby Locke: "We got on famously, and I tell you this I had a three at the difficult ninth in both the morning and afternoon. I think even Nick Faldo would settle for that!"

We shall return to Muirfield later, but Minto holds a special place in Ken's affections: "It's a wonderful course in such a great setting with a super membership and I would do anything for that club. It's very much part of our family." Indeed it is for it was Ken's father who was partly responsible for its establishment back in 1928. The history begins with an approach to the Earl of Minto: "Jim Murray who came from Fife and was a very good golfer was assistant factor on the estate and he asked Lord Minto if he would consider giving up some land for a golf course."

Lord Minto thought it was an excellent idea: "That was it really, we just got on with it and made a brand new course out of old grassland near to Minto House. There was a gang of us who did most of the work and my father would send up the mart staff and the farm staff with horses and carts. Jim Murray was, I suppose, the architect and he directed the carting of stones from the Minto Crags to build the tees and greens. He made a really good job of it and the nine hole course soon became very popular with the locals." Ken has always been one of the keenest members. He has twice been club president and was instrumental in extending the course to a full eighteen holes in 1979. This move attracted a wider membership: "We now have members from all over the district and from much further afield. We even have some from Scandinavia and Germany. They really enjoy playing there."

The most recent development was the opening of a splendid new clubhouse in 1991: "It's a super facility with a wonderful view to the south and the Cheviots and it's now one of the best and friendliest clubs anywhere." With Ken as a member the friendliness and warmth of welcome can be taken for granted and it was not long before the new clubhouse was well and truly christened.

As a golfer Ken played off a handicap of five at Minto: "It's gone up a bit now." However, he is still a sound striker of the ball and will give anyone a good game and great company during that round. He has, by his own admission, played with many highly interesting people both at Minto and Muirfield and readily admits to having initiated many a business deal on the golf course. One involved a substantial hill farm in the Borders: "I was on the first at Muirfield and ahead of us was Lord Whitburgh who, despite being an old man, was both a useful golfer and a very sharp businessman. Well, he must have noticed me playing behind, because the next thing I knew was that Lord Whitburgh was walking down the fairway and saying - 'Now then Oliver, I want that farm at Dykeraw.'"

Such a direct approach did not unnerve Ken: "We would be delighted to receive an offer from you, Sir." After a few moments discussion it was agreed that the pair would meet the following morning at nine o'clock in Ken's office in Hawick. "I arrived at three minutes past only to discover that Lord Whitburgh had been sitting in his Rolls Royce for at least ten minutes!" The deal took less than ten minutes to conclude.

Two of the happiest days in Ken's year revolve around his annual golf outing for his legion of racing friends: "About fifteen years ago I thought it would be a good idea to get some of the racing people together for a couple of days golf and fun in East Lothian." From the start it proved to be a great success, though somewhat testing on certain individuals' livers: "The very first year we had around thirty people and even after the first night I could see the way things were going. Good God, the bill for drinks was over £1,200!"

The cast at these outings is formidable. Indeed it reads like a *Who's Who* of the racing world with Josh Gifford, Jim Wilson, Jim Old, Nicky Henderson, Oliver and Simon Sherwood, Paul Webber, David Minton, Tony Collins, Willie Jenks, Johnny Harrington and Jeff King regular attenders: "On the first day we play at Gullane and then at night we have one of the best dinners you could imagine in the clubhouse. Sometime during the evening, before everyone gets too outrageous, teams of three are arranged to play at Muirfield the following day." But when the racing fraternity are together there has to be an element of gambling: "We auction the teams and whoever buys the winning team scoops the pool."

Bids tend to flow more freely as Ken knows to his cost when the proceedings have been suitably lubricated: "Two years ago I had partaken of too much port and ended up spending rather more money than I should and lost the lot." The following year a different strategy was laid out: "I was bloody sure I wasn't going to buy any teams at all. However, by the time the auction was on I had dozed off but when I woke I found out that the team I was in had been knocked down to me for £82 by David Minton, the noted bloodstock agent. Here we go again I thought!" The outcome, happily, was highly pleasurable: "Heavens above, my team won and I collected £1,250 for my £82."

Some of the participants are more than average golfers - including Oliver and Simon Sherwood, Paul Webber of the Curragh Bloodstock Agency and David Minton - but others are less than proficient. One in that category is Geoff Adam, a director of Kelso Racecourse and owner of that fine chaser, Pat's Jester: "Some years ago Geoff had indulged in a 'very good lunch' so that on the second tee at Muirfield they damned nearly needed a bulldozer to replace the divots he was flinging up!"

The 1993 gathering was a touching one for Ken: "I was so honoured when they presented me with a wonderful picture of Muirfield looking from the thirteenth green back to the clubhouse and away to the Lammermuir Hills. "The presentation was made by Josh Gifford who has also given Ken a picture of the last fence at Cheltenham featuring Deep

1982. Cockle Strand and David Dutton on the way to victory in the Scottish Grand National from another Oliver horse, Three To One, ridden by Jonjo O'Neill.

1991. Part of Ken's noted gardens at Hassendean Bank.

1990. Ken and his dog Tracy in front of the house.

1990. Ken's daughter Susan leading in his grand-daughters Sandy, after a win at the Jedforest Point-to-point on Mossy Moore.

1988. High Edge Grey ridden by Tim Reed on the way to winning the Charlie Hall Memorial Chase at Wetherby.

1990. Ken jumping into swimming pool in Portugal. Unbelievably he was aged over 75 when this photograph was taken.

1993. Josh Gifford presenting Ken with a picture of Muirfield Golf Club.

1993 October. Ken, Jack Berry and Rhona inspecting a yearling at Doncaster Sales.

Sensation on his way to winning the 1993 Queen Mother Champion Chase. Both hang prominently at Hassendean Bank. Ken's love of Muirfield is unquestionable: "I like going through and having a quiet round and a chat with people over a drink because it's so relaxing. Sometimes I have stayed in the clubhouse overnight in the wonderful rooms which they have. There is nothing better in the morning than to get up at about six, open the window and look out over the eighteenth green on what has to be one of the very best courses anywhere in the world. I am so lucky to be a member and to have met an enormous number of friends, some of which go right back to the days when I was at school at Merchiston."

Ken has played golf in many countries and consequently he has met some highly interesting people. One such occasion was many years ago when he was playing in the south of France at Cannes with a Dutch friend: "As we were completing our round we met this tall gentleman who knew my Dutch friend, and we all adjourned for a drink. In the course of the conversation the tall gentleman, knowing of my interest in racing, remarked that he had a son whose horse, the Ministrel, had just won the Derby. The gentleman was of course Vernon Sangster of Vernon's Pools fame and father of Robert." That was the start of a lasting friendship and for the next week Ken played virtually every day with Vernon Sangster and his wife Peggy.

Even as he approaches eighty years of age Ken's appetite for golf is as keen as ever and while on holiday in Portugal he played no less than 170 holes with Padge Berry. His opinion of Padge as a judge of horse flesh is not in doubt but of his golfing prowess he is marginally less complimentary: "He's in too much of a bloody hurry - no patience!"

The Royal Highland and Agricultural Society of Scotland has a history stretching back over 200 years and for most of that time it has been the foremost organisation in Scotland's farming industry, fostering education and higher standards of husbandry. The highlight of the farming year is undoubtedly the Royal Highland Show held in late June in the magnificent setting of Ingliston on Edinburgh's western approaches. Formerly a golf course, the site was purchased for a mere £55,000 in 1958 on the advice of Bob Urquhart, agricultural editor of *The Scotsman*. That investment has proved to be one of the wisest ever made and since the first Highland Show was held at Ingliston in 1960, the whole site has been progressively developed into a natural focus for Scottish agriculture. Only last year the National Farmers Union of Scotland moved from its city centre offices to set up shop at Ingliston and it seems certain that other organisations will follow suit.

The Highland Society is a charitable trust administered by a chief executive who in turn is answerable to a board of directors. To be elected a director is no sinecure and while the entire board have to put their shoulders to the wheel it is a considerable honour to be elected to their number. Ken has been involved with the Highland for many years and, despite his age, he is still one of the most active of all the directors. His fellow directors know that a board meeting will not pass without a contribution from Ken, and in truth his wise words and wisdom have proved invaluable over many years. Indeed, his humour and sharp wit have enlivened some of the drier moments in the board room.

Horses and ponies had always been a major part of the Highland Show, but in 1962, following the death four years previously of Jimmy Patterson, one of the stalwarts of the Scottish equestrian scene and against whom Ken rode in his first point-to-point, the entries had fallen away badly. Obviously something had to be done and some of the directors realised that fresh blood was needed. Ken just happened to be the chosen new blood: "It was Bob Forrest from Preston, Duns, whom I had known for many years who asked me to stand for election to the board."

Duly elected, Ken attended his first board meeting in the Highland's headquarters, which were then in Eglinton Crescent in the heart of Edinburgh: "I was very much the new boy sitting at the back, but I made my views known. I told my fellow directors quite plainly that times were changing and that no-one could any longer afford to come to a show for an entire week and put a groom up for all that time. It just wasn't on. I also told them that we had to get things organised so that most exhibitors could arrive and leave on the same day."

These opinions may seem eminently sensible today but not to everyone then: "I got some awful looks from the old established brigade of fuddy duddies who had been on the board for donkeys years." There was apparently a fair degree of muttering about this young upstart and did he not realise that he was not supposed to speak out at his very first meeting. Some were heard to say: "Who is that fellow anyway? Oliver, the auctioneer, we shouldn't have the likes of him. We'll have to speak to Forrest and tell him to be much more careful in future about who he proposes to the board. Besides that, Oliver will have to learn that he must not speak unless spoken to!"

But there were others who were appreciative, including Dr. James Durno, who was one of the most respected figures in Scottish agriculture for many years: "Dr. Durno came up to me afterwards, put his hand on

154

my shoulder and congratulated me for speaking out," adding that it was high time there was some fresh blood and new ideas. "We need to know what the younger generation are thinking", he said.

New ideas have always flowed from Ken, but to begin with he concentrated on reviving the horse sections at the Highland through sheer hard work and canvassing. His policy worked: "I had a lot of help from my friend Jock Campbell and we worked the thing up until the classes were almost bursting at the seams" Show-jumping was next on the list and here Ken's many connections once more came into play: "Through Willie Stephenson I met the McGrath family who run the famous Irish Hospital Sweepstake. At that time they were very keen on show-jumping and retained Seamus Hayes to ride for them. I got in touch with the McGraths and persuaded them to put up some sponsorship."

The McGraths were only too happy to oblige and put up £1,500, which was in fact the very first sporting sponsorship of its kind in Scotland, strange as it may seem thirty years on when every sporting event has a sponsor. Seamus Hayes duly won that first competition and thereafter all the top riders, including Harvey Smith and David Broome became regulars at the Highland Show. Next on Ken's progression was to be appointed chief steward in the main ring - one of the most important duties of the whole show. "We had some good fun during the twelve years I was in charge, and I managed to get together a parade of famous horses at one particular show. We had Freddie, Sebastian V, Young Ashleaf, What a Myth, Red Rum, Rubstic, King Con, Lucius, Wyndburgh, Tingle Creek and Fighting Fit." That parade, which took a lot of work to organise, was much appreciated by the ringside crowd and indeed put the pressure on Ken to come up with something different the following year.

Needless to say he did: "I laid on a donkey derby with many of the leading National Hunt Jockeys from the North taking part. We had Barry Brogan, Graham Macmillan, Ron Barry, Swannie Haldane, and John Leach to name but a few. A great time was had by all with one enormous party in the Roxburghe Hotel and all expenses paid for the entire show."

Possibly Ken's greatest contribution to the Highland Show was still to come. In conversation with his farmer friend Jimmy Mauchlen at the sales in the mart in Hawick, their mutual love of flowers and gardening in general led them to remark on how far the Flower Show at the Highland had slipped. They resolved to do something about the situation. "We attended a meeting of the Highland Society in Melrose and raised our criticisms. We got absolutely no official encouragement. All we were told was that it was impossible to get flowers to bloom in Scotland in the middle of June.

Of course I knew this to be utter nonsense."

However, the chance came a year later when Ken stepped down from his duties in the main ring and volunteered to take on the Flower Show, but on the condition that he had Jimmy Mauchlen as his assistant. Everyone knew of Ken's love of gardening but they were less sure of Jimmy: "He was one of those larger than life people and he certainly enjoyed a drink, but he was a great friend of mine and I knew we could do the job as a team." Ken got his way and set about making the Flower Show at the Highland into one of the premier shows of its kind in the country.

Running the Flower Show necessitated travelling around the country to similar events to canvass potential exhibitors and to keep in contact with the regulars. Southport was one fixture on the itinerary: "Jimmy and I went down together although we had a driver with us, just in case. However, we split up and did our work arranging to meet up again at lunchtime. It was a boiling hot day, so we decided to go and have a small refreshment. The trouble was we walked for miles and couldn't find a bar or anywhere at all that would give us a drink." The Oliver ingenuity yet again took over: "Poor Jimmy was beginning to suffer, so I said - come on we'll go into the National Westminster Bank Stand." The introductions were duly made and Ken and Jimmy were ushered through to the back of the stand where they were made more than welcome with a large gin and tonic for Ken and a large whisky for Jimmy.

Just then Percy Thrower, the famous television gardener of many years, walked in. He took one look at the pair and said "My God, it's you two. I just cannot keep up with you when I come to Ingliston." Much mirth ensued, then Ken added: "Well, Percy I'm going to tell you a story against Jimmy and myself. Just after our last Highland Show two old women were heard to remark, did you see the Flower Show at the Highland. It was tremendous. In fact it's the best show I've ever seen and to think it's run by a pair of alcoholics!"

The return journey from Southport was not uneventful, and it was certainly prudent that a driver had been engaged for the day. Ken remembers it all vividly: "We decided to leave after our chat with Percy Thrower, but it was very hot so we decided to stop at Cannonbie, just over the Scottish border, for another refreshment at about five o'clock in the afternoon. I rang Rhona and explained what a marvellous day we had had, what hard work we had done and that we would be home by about half past seven." Rhona was slightly puzzled by this estimated time of arrival because under normal driving conditions Cannonbie to

Hassendean Bank should take no longer than an hour. "What are you going to be doing for the next two and a half hours?" enquired Rhona. Ken takes up the tale: "We'd given ourselves a deadline, and I have never seen so much whisky or gin consumed in so short a time, but we got home bang on time!"

Not many years later Jimmy Mauchlen died at the early age of fifty, and Ken still misses him: "I am sorry that Jimmy is not alive today to see how successful the Flower Show has become. He would have been delighted with the way it has developed, and a fair proportion of that credit is due to him. He liked fun but he never missed out on the hard work when it was called for." The Flower Show has indeed become a major part of the Highland Show and is now widely recognised as easily the best in Scotland and the north of England. Trade exhibitors regularly say that they do more business at the Highland than at other shows, and certainly all of them know Ken. He really has been 'Mr. Flower Show' for many years.

Ken was a director of the Highland non-stop for thirty years and thoroughly enjoyed every moment of it: "If I have done anything at all for the Highland I have been more than rewarded by the enormous number of people I have met and the friendships made in the boardroom and at the shows over the years." Two years ago Ken was made an Honorary Vice-President of the Royal Highland and Agricultural Society of Scotland, and it is an honour of which he is deeply proud: "I was so touched, and while I am semi-retired and without a vote in the meetings it is nice that people ask my opinion on various matters."

The board hold regular meeting throughout the year and Ken now travels in with his friend and near neighbour Charles Scott who has gradually assumed many of the duties undertaken by Ken: "Charles is a very hard working director and I enjoy going to the meetings with him." In turn Charles says of his mentor: "I don't know where he gets all the energy from. You would think that at his age he would want a quieter life, but not a bit of it. He wants to be involved in everything."

Charles Scott is one of those characters who is very diffident and modest regarding his own achievements, but Ken knows just exactly what he has accomplished: "Charles was a great amateur rider and won the Foxhunter at Liverpool on Merryman II before the horse went on the next year to win the Grand National, although Charles gave up the ride to allow the connections to engage a professional after his win at Liverpool. He always keeps a good horse about him and loves nothing better than to buy young horses in Ireland and turn them over at Doncaster."

The current chairman of the Highland Society is Tommy Dun, another of Ken's legion of friends. "I suppose I got to know Tommy and his brother Robin years ago when they were just boys and came to Hawick to sell their North Country Cheviot lambs at the mart. I've known the Dun family ever since - and we're now talking about a third generation." Tommy and his brother Robin had a reputation for being rather wild in their youth, and indeed there are some who say that nothing much has changed over the years. Tommy in particular has long held a keen interest in the affairs of the Highland Show and for an extended period was the senior sheep steward before being appointed chairman in November 1992.

Ken has no doubts about his abilities: "Tommy is one of those amazing characters who you might think would never be able to do anything, but it's quite the reverse. He really gets things done and stands absolutely no nonsense in meetings." The firm friendship between Tommy and Ken extends to some of Ken's horses grazing during the summer months at Tommy's farm at Nether Brotherstone where they always seem to enjoy the freedom of the hills and the change of air. Meanwhile Tommy's wife, Jackie, is herself steeped in racing, having been a very successful point-to-point rider in the mid-1950's with such horses as Dunboy and Spud Tamson. Both were great favourites on the point-to-point and hunter chase circuit, but the greatest occasion of all was at the Cheltenham Festival meeting in 1958 when Spud Tamson, trained by Tommy and ridden by her brother-in-law Robin, won the National Hunt Chase. The next day Jackie's twin sister Jill saw her horse, Whinstone Hill, win the Foxhunters. In turn Tommy and Jackie are the proud parents of Geordie who rode for Ken and of Peter who was well on his way to being a top-flight jockey before an accident at Hexham put an end to his career. As Ken says with a rueful smile: "The Duns are great people, and it's rather like a good line of horses - you've got to get the breeding right."

Tommy Dun's immediate predecessor as Chairman of the Highland Society was the Aberdeenshire farmer Jack Sleigh and he and Ken are firm friends. Indeed it was through Jack that Ken met one of the richest men in the world, Steve Forbes of the *Forbes Magazine* and publishing empire. Steve Forbes' father Malcolm had left Aberdeenshire at the turn of the century to make his fortune in the New World, and that he did, meeting the likes of Andrew Carnegie and John D. Rockefeller. Jack Sleigh thought it would be a good idea to ask Steve Forbes to be the Honorary President of the Highland Show in 1992.

Ken and his fellow directors fell in with the idea and were delighted when Mr. Forbes agreed. To persuade a man of such wealth to come to Edinburgh was quite something, and he did not let anyone down. In fact he arrived in his own private Boeing jet with its name - the Capitalist Tool - emblazoned along the fuselage. Steve Forbes soon impressed everyone, including Ken: "He might be one of the richest men in the world, but you would never guess it. When I met him he was rather shy, but you could tell that his mind was as sharp as a razor with an interest in everything that was happening." A substantial donation to the Highland's funds was one result of that visit, but as Ken put it: "We knew we had met one of the great men of the world."

Another former chairman, Fraser Morrison, is a firm friend of Ken: "Fraser and I had great fun over many years, and I was so pleased when his son Ian won his first rugby cap for Scotland in 1993." Fraser, who is one of the most accomplished after dinner speakers anywhere in the country, has his own particular way with words when it comes to Ken and his lifestyle: "That man Oliver is a bloody miracle. Anyone else who tried to do half what he has done would have been knackered years ago. The old bugger just keeps going on."

In one sense it is a wonder that Ken ever rose to the exalted heights of being a director, for way back in 1938, when the Highland Show was held in Dumfries, a certain young Oliver was up to high jinks: "There was a crowd of us and they caught me and put me in a pig crate and wheeled me around the showground. That was bad enough but we collided with the directors stand and knocked some railings down. There was a bit of a row about that!"

Ken obviously enjoys the Highland Show enormously and now that his duties are less onerous he has more time to meet many of his friends both old and young. In 1993 he had a particular tale to tell relating to his son Stuart and daughter-in-law Ann who were at the time living at Hassendean Bank while their new house was being completed. "They've got this bloody big black dog. And do you know what the devil did - he ate my false teeth!" Indeed he did, but over the years Ken has got his teeth into the Highland and few would dispute that the show is not all the better for that.

159

11

THE 1990's

Retirement is a word that never passes the lips of Ken Oliver. He quite simply will never retire. His whole life has been one where the interplay between genuine work and a whole range of other activities has never been marked out in black and white. In short it has been a life full to the brim with action and fun and one where those who have known Ken have been enriched enormously.

Throughout the great training years of the mid-1960's and into the 1970's the business of Andrew Oliver and Son Limited continued to prosper with considerable benefits for the farming community in the locality. The mart in Hawick was the very first to instal a weighbridge so that all store stock - young cattle and sheep sold by their breeders for further fattening - could be auctioned with purchasers having an accurate indication of just how much they were paying for each kilo. The concept was welcomed by all progressive farmers, though there were one or two of the old diehards who thought it would take away much of the mystique of marketing. However, the proof of Ken's wisdom can be seen today in every substantial auction mart in the country. Few buyers would consider buying cattle or sheep unless they knew the weight of the consignment in front of the ringside.

The Hawick area has always been one renowned for its sheep, but Ken soon came to appreciate that successive Governments were actively encouraging farmers to give more consideration to beef production through the introduction of a wide range of subsidies - most notably the Hill Cow Subsidy. The result of this 'carrot' was that large numbers of breeding cattle began to appear on the hills where formerly sheep had grazed alone. This had a twin effect. Firstly there was a keen, if not almost insatiable demand, from all over the country for quality breeding stock. Secondly the product of that breeding stock had to be marketed. Andrew Oliver and Son Limited were at the forefront of both facets. The expertise of the Border farmer is second to none and soon large sales of breeding cattle were being held each autumn in Hawick where the famous Blue Grey heifers, which are the result of crossing a White Shorthorn bull with a Galloway cow, experienced an enormous demand.

Buyers arrived in Hawick in early November from literally all over Britain determined to have their Blue Grey heifers from the Border country. The principal sale invariably fell on the first Thursday in November and from nine in the morning for the next ten or twelve hours the ring was a hive of activity. All categories of breeding stock were sold, but as with the bloodstock industry it was the youngsters - the heifers ready to be bred - which were the stars of the day. Occasionally it would be late in the proceedings before this section was reached, but this was Ken's hour. He would watch his team of auctioneers in action all day, but this was the time for the master to assume the rostrum.

Prices were almost always on the up in those days, and the cause for a celebration or two afterwards. Ken has, to say the very least, some fond memories: "They were great times, but above all I remember Walter Elliot of Kirndean. Walter was universally known as Tat and he was a huge man, but when he brought his first heifers into the ring one year I was in for a mighty shock - he suddenly pulled out a bottle of champagne from under his coat, popped the cork and presented me with a glass!"

That gesture had the ringside rocking with laughter, and it just happened to give the sale an extra boost. Not every buyer managed to find the breeding stock he required at one of the sales and so Ken and his team built up a very large private treaty business, whereby cattle were bought straight from farms and transferred to new owners without ever going through the ring. In one sense this was an easy business and operated on a much lower cost basis, but it was totally dependent on trust all round. The vendor had to be sure in his own mind that he was getting a fair price, while at the same time the purchaser, who might well be hundreds of miles away, had to have confidence that the cattle sent to him unseen represented value for money.

Some auctioneers are infinitely better than others, no matter what they are selling. Ken has seen a few in his time: "I would say they are born or bred to the job. You can attempt to train someone but unless they have it in them they will never be any better than average." One such lad who was clearly born to the profession was Michael Stanners. Back in the early

1970's Johnny Marshall who farmed at Cherrytrees, near Yetholm, said: "Look Ken, one of my shepherds has been at me to see if you might have a place in the mart for his son. He's a bright spark with a lot of go and he really wants to be an auctioneer. I think he might just fit in with you."

That was it. A diminutive young lad from Northumberland arrived at Hawick and as did Ken in his time, started right at the very bottom of the pile. "Michael was always full of energy and tremendously keen to have a go at anything. I soon knew he would make it and gave him every encouragement I possibly could, while at the same time I tried to restrain him from being just that bit too pushy". The old master and the young trainee hit it off right from the start, and although Michael moved to Norfolk a few years ago he still regularly returns to the Borders and never ceases in his genuine affection for the man who started him on the road to success: "He taught me so much and introduced me to so many people. Apart from that we had great fun together."

Selling the ultimate product of those breeding cattle was an opportunity not to be missed and soon Hawick mart was one of the principal centres each October for suckled calves. The cattle were in the region of six to ten months of age and had just been weaned, ready to go on for fattening in more favourable parts of the country. The sales at Hawick grew to a vast scale under Ken's stewardship: "At one time we undoubtedly held the largest sale with approaching 10,000 head spread over three full days. It was a colossal operation attracting both buyers and sellers from far and near". It was also an opportunity for Ken to do business in more than one field: "It was amazing what might happen after a sale when we retired to the bar. I would get talking to people and before you knew it I would discover they had an interest in racing. More than once that ended up with a new owner in the yard."

The farming world was, however, changing and not necessarily to the benefit of Andrew Oliver and Son Limited. Tax concessions were encouraging individuals who were paying income tax at the very top of the scale to invest in forestry so as to protect their capital and largely avoid inheritance and capital gains taxes. The result was that vast tracts of the Border hills were cleared of sheep and submerged under a blanket of anonymous Sitka spruce. The legacy of that largely unplanned afforestation is horribly visible in deserted valleys all over the Borders. Borthwick Water, Eskdalemuir and Liddesdale now support very few viable farms. The people have gone. The cottages formerly occupied by shepherds are now holiday homes lived in but for a short time each summer. The sheep and cattle have also gone, and so too the need for marketing.

Indeed the whole pattern of livestock marketing was beginning to change. Farmers who traditionally sold their sheep and cattle as stores were now increasingly keeping them on to a later stage or selling direct to abattoirs. This meant that whereas in the old days an auctioneer might see the same stock pass through his hands twice, or even three times, he was now lucky to have one slice of commission. The perceived wisdom among desk-bound farming experts was that sheep did not pay on low-ground farms. Hence there was a decline in the demand from breeding stock from such traditional sources as the Hawick area. Bad news indeed for Andrew Oliver and Son Limited.

Ken passed the traditional age of retirement at sixty-five with no thoughts of winding down, though there was one very great party, when he was presented with a silver salver from his many friends. However, over the next five years he could see that if Hawick was to have a mart it would have to be as part of a larger concern so that costs could be more widely spread. The chance came with an approach from the Edinburgh based firm of Oliver and Son Limited. This was a strange coincidence but one which Ken truly welcomed: "The Edinburgh firm was started by my grandfather as an adjunct to the business in Hawick to serve farmers in the Lothians and Fife. It was very successful but in 1898 he decided to sell out on the condition that Oliver and Son were disqualified from selling livestock in the county of Roxburghshire."

Many years ago Ken's father, Douglas, noticed a breach in this agreement: "Father spotted that Oliver and Son Limited were selling rams at the Kelso Ram Sales, so he took the matter up with them through the courts. The result was that they would be allowed to continue to sell, but that after the deduction of expenses, all commission income should be split on an equal basis." Douglas Oliver was certainly a shrewd operator but Ken was equally astute and a mutually acceptable deal was arrived at resulting in Oliver and Son Limited taking control of Andrew Oliver and Son Limited. Ken benefitted financially and was retained on a consultancy basis. But the main objective in his mind was clear: "I wanted the mart to remain in Hawick for the farming community because it was needed."

For a few years everything went well, but then a predator appeared on the scene in the form of Lawrie and Symington Limited, the Lanark based auctioneers who were determined to expand their business base. They acquired control of Oliver and Son Limited and, despite some very deter-mined local opposition, the mart in Hawick. Logic would have suggested that this would be a good move for farmers in that Lawrie and Symington were one of the largest and most successful companies in the country.

However, life is not that simple. A series of management and boardroom changes resulted in business in Hawick slipping badly with the mart eventually being sold to a property developer for £1.5 million. That developer promptly sold it on again to a supermarket, making a profit in excess of £1 million overnight. It was a sorry affair and one that left a bitter taste, not least with Ken: "It makes me sick to think of what happened and what a mess certain people made of everything." To his credit however, throughout the whole affair, Ken refrained from comment but it was a sorry day for him when the bulldozers moved into the mart to make way for the supermarket. Hawick mart in its day was a wonderful market of a different and less controversial pedigree.

On a much happier note Ken has always had a great interest in sporting pictures and in recent times this interest has reached a new peak: "I just love having good pictures around me and many of the ones at Hassendean Bank have a particular tale to tell". Indeed they do, and several are by that most favoured of sporting artists, Lionel Edwards: "He came to stay in 1962 and stayed for a fortnight. I gave him several introductions, including to the Misses Roberston of Cutty Sark whisky who of course were great racing people and had a whole string of good horses with Bobby Fairbairn." While staying with Ken and Rhona, Lionel Edwards painted both Wyndburgh and Sanvina as well as "a super picture of the Kelso horse sales with my old friends Alistair Paton and Alec Tully in the foreground."

All three occupy pride of place at Hassendean Bank as well as several others by the same artist and have a value beyond financial price. However, Ken had a recent insight into what they might fetch on the open market: "After the Misses Robertsons died there was a huge sale of their effects including some Lionel Edwards paintings so I thought I would have a look at them. They all made over £6,000 each. Lionel charged me £350 in total for the three he painted when he stayed. He really was a super chap and I used to sit by the fireside and listen to his tales of hunting with over eighty packs of hounds all over the world. I just love his pictures and would never sell them."

The famous Border artist Tom Scott is another of Ken's favourites, especially a massive scene depicting the Duke of Buccleuch's hounds moving off from a meet at Riddell, near Selkirk. It is a picture which has been much admired, not least by several Dukes of Buccleuch: "It came here from my mother's side of the family and was painted over a hundred years ago. The present Duke's grandfather tried very hard to buy it from my father, but he just would not part with it and neither would I."

Several other Tom Scotts hang prominently, including one of Scotland's oldest continuously inhabited house, Traquair, near Innerleithen. The scene is an emotive one of Bonnie Prince Charlie passing through the great Golden gates. Those gates were afterwards closed and have never been opened since, nor ever will be until a Stuart resumes the throne of Great Britain. However, the picture which has given Ken most delight in recent times is the one presented to him of Muirfield Clubhouse by his racing friends. Secretary of the Honourable Company of Edinburgh Golfers is John Prideaux - also involved in a syndicate which has a horse in training with Ken - and he said of it: "It must be one of the best pictures ever painted of Muirfield and I know just how much it is appreciated."

Many of the outstanding winners from Hassendean Bank are portrayed on canvas, including one of Rhona galloping Even Keel. Others include Fighting Fit and one of the famous five winners at Wolverhampton. The Oliver character has also been captured in some style by local artist Margaret Peach in a portrait presented to Ken by his friends on the occasion of his sixty-fifth birthday. Memories do indeed hang in profusion from the walls and jump straight out of the scrapbooks which have so dutifully been updated over the years. Similarly the bookshelves are stocked with a profusion of titles ranging from gardening to local history. On the latter count, there is one book which Ken especially treasures: "It's all about the history of the Buccleuch family and the history of the locality and was written by my grandmother." She must have been a remarkable lady for it was she who gave the address when in 1902 a memorial was unveiled at Hornshole, just outside Hawick, commemorating the exploits of the young men, or Callants, of Hawick, who in 1514 - the year after the slaughter of the Scottish army at the Battle of Flodden - routed a band of English troops and captured their standard. Their deeds are celebrated each year at the Hawick Common Ridings.

Family ties and kinship lie close to the heart of the Borderer and Ken is certainly no exception. Justly proud of his family and their achievements, as they are in turn of him, though they regularly express surprise, not to say downright amazement at the stamina of the head of the family. Daughter Susan was born in 1942 and has "an absolute passion for fox-hunting." Susan also joined a sporting family when she married Billy Forster who farmed just up the road at Hassendean. Billy was an excellent amateur rider in the 1950's winning many point-to-points and hunter chases, most notably on his mare Cousin Kate. Sadly that marriage was dissolved but the next generation have given their grandfather much to enrichen his later years. "My oldest grand-daughter, Nicola, has travelled virtually all over the world and is in great demand as an organiser of house parties and for entertainment."

Number two grand-daughter Sandy clearly must have inherited the thrill of the chase for she marked herself out as one of the outstanding lady riders of recent times, winning many races on Mossy Moor. Grandfather, not unsurprisingly, had a hand in her success: "Mossy Moore was bought by David Minton, the bloodstock agent, for a client. We had him in the yard and won several good races with him. However, his heart went wrong, but he was such a grand horse that we kept him on and Rhona rode him quite a bit, using him as a lead horse for some of the younger ones in the stable. He was a grand schoolmaster."

Young Sandy was "quite horse mad" and when she went down south to Henrietta Knight's famous point-to-point yard she persuaded her grandfather to let her take Mossy Moore for company. Before anyone could blink, young Sandy had won a point-to-point on this horse with a supposedly dodgy heart. The following season Sandy and Mossy were back in the Borders at Alan Mactaggart's yard where Alan and his wife Marty proved to be so good with both Sandy and her beloved "Mossy."

Hunting with the Jedforest was the ideal preparation for the rejuvenated Mossy Moore and almost from the start of the Northern point-to-point circuit Sandy was winning week after week. No-one was more delighted than Ken, and the sight of him running towards the winner's enclosure one Saturday at Ratheugh, near Alnwick, to greet Sandy after a particularly hard race was one that brought a smile to many a face. Since then Sandy has immersed herself in the equestrian world working with, among others, David Nicholson. No-one would be surprised if at some future date young Sandy did not seek to emulate her illustrious grandfather by becoming a trainer in her own right.

Grandson Clive Forster is, however, very much the farmer, gradually taking charge of the day-to-day side of things on the land at Hassendean Bank. Clive is a thoroughly practical young man who has a sense of humour that suggests its roots in the Oliver side of his pedigree, although he is less keen on horses than his sisters. Ken remembers one day when Clive was younger and one of the stable's owners, Peter Cameron, was visiting: "As ever there was a degree of fun and we even had Peter dressed up with a jockey's cap up on old Drumikill watched by Peter's son and Clive. Rhona at this stage turned to Clive and asked - well, which one do you like? He was quick - none of them!"

Ken's son Stuart was born in 1947 and like his father was educated at Merchiston Castle in Edinburgh. After leaving school Stuart was sent to learn the auctioneering profession with one of the all-time greats, Roley Fraser in Perth, who in his time sold some of the highest priced beef bulls in the world at the internationally renowned Perth Bull Sales. Stuart then returned to Hawick and joined the family firm where he soon developed his own style, his zest for life frequently terrifying the wits out anyone who dared to sit beside him as a passenger in a succession of fast cars that he seemed able to make go faster than anyone else.

Stuart also had the knack of making horses run fast enough to win a not inconsiderable share of races under his jockeyship, much to the great pride of his father: "He was a useful jockey and I well remember him winning on Kara Sea, and of course on his own horse - The Benign Bishop." Over the years, despite being involved with Andrew Oliver and Son and at Doncaster, Stuart began to develop new interests and now he is totally involved with the construction industry through Oliver Homes Limited, based in the Burnfoot Industrial Estate in Hawick.

The company was founded twenty years ago with the objective of supplying kit-type timber-framed houses for the top end of the market. Ken takes a keen interest in the company: "The last two years, as everyone in this business knows full well have been very difficult, but things are picking up now and there are definite signs of expansion." The current turnover is in the region of £2.5 million and Ken is very proud of the fact that "we have sold houses from the south-east of England right up to the Shetlands." Stuart and his wife Ann moved into one of their own products in mid-1993, just north of the farmhouse at Hassendean Bank, and Ken quite clearly enjoys having them in such close proximity.

Of all the attributes to a long and successful life, enduring good health has to be foremost. As far as his riding days were concerned Ken was remarkably lucky, suffering very few falls and no serious injuries. The war was less kind to him, but back in his home environment his recovery was soon total. However, the pace began to tell towards Ken's seventy-fifth birthday: "I was having some trouble with angina and after consultation with Dr. John Gaddy at the Borders General Hospital I was strongly advised to have a heart by-pass operation." Prior to that advice Ken had a brief stay in Scotland's leading private hospital, the Murrayfield in Edinburgh: "It was a delightful place and the consultant was very good to me, telling me that I should have the operation. I agreed and was told that I could be operated on the following Monday at a private clinic in Glasgow."

That sounded ideal, but Ken's mind moved on: "I asked what the cost would be and was told that the operation would cost me £10,000". Ken was not having that: "You're not on at all. I could buy a decent horse for that!" The benefits of the National Health Service soon became obvious: "John Gaddy fixed it up for me to be operated on by that marvellous surgeon, Christopher Sang, in the Edinburgh Royal Infirmary. I went in on a Friday for the operation the following Monday morning. On the Sunday Mr. Sang came into to see me with a huge chart and announced that he was going to give me four by-passes the following morning. Ken was marginally alarmed at this prospect: "Do you not think you are overdoing things a bit? The answer soon put Ken in his place: "When I'm in I'm going to put the plumbing right." Ken had great confidence in his surgeon and soon the pair were engaged in banter with Ken making the running: "Fair enough, but there is one thing which worries me. We were both educated in Edinburgh. You were at George Watson's while I went to Merchiston Castle. That worries me a bit, because while we were great rivals, we nearly always slaughtered you!"

Happily, the five hour operation was a great success and the patient was out of the intensive care unit on the day after surgery. Dan Buglass, knows full well how rapid was that recovery, for on returning from Aberdeen on the Wednesday evening he looked in at the Royal Infirmary with a request to see Ken for "just a few minutes." The ward sister was unconcerned: "You can stay for as long as you like. Mr. Oliver is virtually running the ward." And so it appeared, for there he was sitting by his bed reading *The Sporting Life!*"

At the beginning of the following week Ken was transferred back to the Borders General Hospital in Melrose and on the Wednesday celebrated his seventy-fifth birthday with a string of visitors, most of whom arrived bearing bottles of champagne. He was allowed home on the Friday morning, and again Dan Buglass, knows exactly how rapid was Ken's recovery for he brought Andy Goram, the Scotland and Glasgow Rangers goal-keeper, to see him with a view to the footballer acquiring an interest in a horse. It was a bitterly cold February morning, but Ken's spirits were high, and despite protests from Rhona he insisted on going to Kelso Races that very afternoon to see the two horses from the stable which were running that day. Everyone at Kelso was amazed at the man's constitution, but that was not the end of his exploits - he even stopped in for a few minutes on the way home at the Fox and Hounds in Denholm to thank the many people who had wished him well.

The stories which followed that transformation in Ken's health are legion. One which he tells himself related to his fondness for Tio Pepe sherry and the fact that he had had a quadruple by-pass: "Three for the blood and one for the Tio Pepe." On another occasion while enjoying a quiet drink with his friend Dr. Rory Hamilton in the Conservative Club, Ken remarked how well he was feeling, adding: "You know this, Rory. When I die, which I might add will not be for many years yet, I'm going to leave all my organs for transplant." Rory looked staggered for a moment, then had a quick and deep slug at his drink, before commenting: "Well Kenneth, I pity the chap who wakes up with your liver, because he will certainly come to with one helluva hangover!"

Jokes apart, Ken is forever grateful to the medical profession, and not just on account of what they did for his heart: "They really did put me right, but with one very interesting side effect. I used to have a hearing aid in both ears, but one day about a month after the operation I didn't have them in and it suddenly struck me that I had recovered virtually all my hearing. That was some bonus." The experts in the Royal Infirmary were astounded at this news and told Ken that he has now well and truly entered the annals of medical history. It is not the first time he has been in a record book, but this must be one that he never anticipated even in his wildest dreams. Chronic asthma had been another problem, but that is now largely cured thanks to a ventilator used night and morning: "We use the same equipment on the horses and it works for them too."

Sound in wind and heart and still as full of enthusiasm for life as ever Ken Oliver is a man who defies the norms of life in every sense. He still trains a dozen or so horses, hankering yet for that great horse and, who knows, a win still in the Grand National. Justice would be served by that eventuality. The pleasure he gains from breeding from the Sanvina line is undiminished and even when things go wrong the complaints are few: "I've had my share of luck in the past." The trips to Muirfield or the quiet round at Minto are still regular features of his life, while his garden is another joy. Asked recently why he persisted in growing so many vegetables when the household consists of just Rhona and himself the reply was interesting: "I know there is far too much here, but I just like watching things grow." And he can still make flowers grow like few others.

Ken has made things grow all his life from the mart, to Doncaster, to his racing career enriching all who have met him. However, the path might have been different without Rhona at his side for so many years: "She has been the most marvellous wife trying to keep me right, which has, I know, never been easy. We've had a great time together."

Friendship has been at the centre of Ken's life and it sustains him yet in the same way as his friendship has supported so many in diverse walks of life. There are many people who have benefitted from unasked and unheralded acts of kindness to which he will add no comment other than a quiet smile. It is these many friendships that Ken has relished most in life: "Everything else counts for little unless you have friends. I've had a bit of fun along the way and the odd success here and there, but it's the people that count at the end of the day."

As the preparations for this book were being finalised Ken turned and said, quoting the great American golfer Bobby Jones when he was given the freedom of St. Andrews: "Friends and friendship I feel sincerely are the most important words in the English language. Friends are a man's priceless treasures and a life rich in friendship is full indeed."

THE HORSES
[APPENDIX]

ARCTIC SUNSET
Brown Gelding.
1960.
By Arctic Slave - Goldenstown.
Probably the horse with the most ability ever trained at Hassendean Bank, Arctic Sunset came over from Ireland having won his only two races there when trained by Paddy Sleator - a Bumper at Gowran Park and the Saggart Hurdle at Naas.

As soon as he arrived with the Olivers, he was put to novice chasing and in November, 1965 he easily won a Novice Chase at Newcastle and followed this up with an impressive performance at Sandown when winning the Henry VIII Chase. His third win in a row was the Cotswold Chase at the National Hunt Festival (now the Arkle Chase) over two miles. In all of these races he was ridden by George Milburn.

The next season Arctic Sunset won the Supreme Novices Chase at Haydock in November and was third in the Champion Two Mile Chase (now the Queen Mother Chase) at the Festival.

The following season he was second in the Mackeson over two-and-a-half miles in November, 1967 but was tragically killed at Sandown early the next year. Arctic Sunset was a lovely ride and was normally ridden out by Ken.

BILLY BOW
Bay Gelding.
1962
By BowSprit - Mrs Josser.
A useful novice hurdler, Billy Bow won three consecutive races in the season 1968/69. Having been unsuccessfully sent novice chasing, it transpired that his wind was going so he was hobdayed. In the 1968/69 season, Billy Bow was sent handicap hurdling with great success, winning five consecutive races, four carrying a penalty. His last win was in the Ladbroke Hurdle at Newcastle carrying 12st. 4lbs. to victory. Tragically he collapsed and died just a few yards after the winning post.

He was a very popular horse with the public and a race named in his honour is now run at Newcastle.

THE BENIGN BISHOP
Bay Gelding.
1967.
By Arctic Slave - Honeytown.
Another very good horse from the Sanvina line. He was given by Ken to his son Stuart, who quite often rode him. In 1971/72, his first season, he won three novice hurdles but proved a very much better chaser and the following season he won five chases, including the Champion Novice Chase at Ayr on 14th March, 1973 and the Champion Novice Chase at Chepstow on 23rd March. The next season he won seven times out of fourteen runs, including the valuable Greenall Whitley at Haydock.

The Benign Bishop was really nice chaser who won on sixteen occasions and was placed another ten times. He is also famous as being the originator of our hero's nickname.

CHANDIGAR
Chestnut Gelding.
1964.
By Autumn Gold - Honeytown.
Bred by Ken from his great Sanvina line, he was given as a young horse to Ken's daughter Susan Forster. A brilliant jumper like Deep Sensation, his close relation trained by Josh Gifford to win this year's Queen Mother Two Mile Champion Chase, he was just short of Gold Cup class according to Ken.

In all Chandigar ran fifty-five times, winning on twenty-one occasions - one hurdle and twenty chases - and was placed another twelve times. His best wins were over two-and-three-quarter miles at Stratford when he won the Roddy Baker Gold Cup in May 1971 and 1975, beating the course record on one occasion.

COCKLE STRAND
Chestnut Gelding.
1973.
By Prince Hansel - Artella.
A winner of a Bumper in Ireland as a six-year-old, Cockle Strand was offered for sale at Doncaster in August, 1980. He was purchased by the popular Scottish racing figure, Colonel David Greig.

Ken, who was conducting the auction, said: "I have in front of me a future winner of the Scottish Grand National". Prophetic words indeed as Cockle Strand won the race twenty months later at Ayr, beating another Oliver horse in Three To One. He was ridden by David Dutton. In all Cockle Strand won five chases.

DRUMIKILL
Bay Gelding.
1961.
By Pampered King - Owen Beg.
A beautifully bred horse by the highly successful chasing sire, Pampered King out of a mare called Owen Beg, who came from an excellent Irish racing family. Drumikill was purchased by Ken as a three-year-old from Padge Berry who remarked, when they were looking at him, "that horse could win a Champion Hurdle you know". In 1969 he very nearly did.

Rhona says of him: "He had an excellent record. He ran sixty-eight times for us, winning on eighteen occasions - eleven hurdles and seven chases and was placed another twenty-four times".

In 1965/66, his first season, Drumikill ran six times and was placed on four occasions. The following season he won a couple of small hurdle races, one at Catterick and one at Wetherby, and improved greatly in his third season at Hassendean Bank, winning five hurdle races including the very valuable Liverpool Hurdle on the 30th March, 1968 at the Aintree Grand National Meeting.

The 1968/69 season proved to be most successful. He started off with a win at Wolverhampton on 11th November when he was one of five Oliver winners that day. However, very much his best run ever was in the Champion Hurdle of 1969 when he led approaching the last flight, which he took by the roots, and finished second to the great Persian War.

In October, 1970 he won his first four Novice Chases at Hexham, Carlisle, Nottingham and Market Rasen. A tough horse and highly successful.

EVEN KEEL
Brown Gelding.
1962.
By Even Money - Officers Pet.
Another tough and successful horse with a good chasing pedigree, Even Keel was purchased by Ken from Padge Berry on the same day he bought Drumikill.

In 1965/66, his first season he ran a couple of times unplaced over hurdles but came good with a vengeance the following season when he won five hurdles on the trot - four Novice Hurdles and a Handicap Hurdle. In the 1966/67 season he started off by winning three handicap hurdle by mid-November at Wetherby, Ayr and Nottingham. He was third at the Cheltenham Festival.

1968/69 proved yet another good season for Even Keel who by this time had become very popular with the public, as he always ran with great fire. He was a difficult horse and easier to control with a neck strap and voice than reins. Rhona normally rode him at work at home and she complains that her shoulders still ache! Even Keel started off the season by winning three Novice Chases at Wolverhampton, Carlisle and Doncaster in November, and a Handicap Chase at Ayr in January. So highly regarded was Even Keel, that instead of being put in a Novice Chase at the National Hunt Festival, he was entered in the Two Mile Champion Chase (now the Queen Mother Two Mile Chase) when he ran an extremely good race to be second to Muir, trained by Tom Dreaper.

The 1969/70 season saw Even Keel win five races including the valuable Billy Bow Ladbroke Hurdle at Newcastle on 8th November, 1969 and four chases, although on two occasions he refused to race. Whether this was due to his disenchantment with racing or the fact that his regular jockey, Barry Brogan, had been paid to stop him is not known, but what better way of stopping a horse than getting it to refuse to race?

Even Keel's two biggest wins over fences came in the closing seasons of his career when he won the Benson & Hedges Gold Cup in December, 1970 at Sandown under 12st. 3lbs. and the Kirk & Kirk Chase over three miles at Ascot in November 1971.

In all Even Keel ran on fifty-eight occasions, winning ten hurdles and thirteen chases and was placed on fourteen occasions. He was a great tribute to the Olivers' ability to keep a horse sound, as tearaways like him are particularly prone to injury on their home training ground as well as on the course itself.

In the end Even Keel got bored with racing and ended up brilliantly hunting hounds with Edmund Vestey in Essex which he loved.

FIGHTING FIT
Brown Gelding.
1972.
By Harwell-Trimblestown Lady.
In his first two seasons, Fighting Fit won three hurdle races but proved a very much better chaser. In the 1978/79 season he ran nine times over fences, winning on six occasions, the last time being the prestigious Scottish Grand National at Ayr over four miles on 21st April, 1979. This was an impressive performance for a novice against seasoned chasers at the end of a hard season.

The next season Fighting Fit won the Hennessy at Newbury in November 1979. In all he won eight chases and three hurdle races.

FORT ROUGE
Chestnut Gelding.
1958.
By Fortina-Golden Sunset.
Fort Rouge by Fortina, (one of the few entires ever to win the Gold Cup) was a very precocious horse. A half-brother to Arctic Sunset he won a three-year-old hurdle at Kelso, but broke down when running well in the Victor Lordorum at Haydock as a four-year-old. He was rested and afterwards proved a useful chaser, winning the Grand Annual under 11st. at Cheltenham's 1965 Festival.

HAPPY ARTHUR
Bay Gelding.
1957.
By Artist's Son-Hopeful Lady.
One of the horses which helped establish the Olivers as leading trainers Happy Arthur won twelve races, seven hurdles and five chases.

His biggest win was in the George Duller over three miles at the Cheltenham National Hunt Festival in March 1963. He ran another great race in April 1965 when he was second over four miles to Brasher in the Scottish Grand National.

HIGH EDGE GREY
Grey Gelding.
1981.
By Precipice Wood-China Bank.
Purchased as a three-year-old at the Doncaster Sales, High Edge Grey developed into a first class chaser, best remembered for his spectacular jumping. High Edge Grey needed time to develop, but when he came good at the beginning of the 1988 season, he was one of the best chasers in training. He started off by winning a couple of nice races at Kelso and then won the highly prestigious Charlie Hall Memorial Pattern Chase at Wetherby. In all three races he was ridden by Tim Reed. He started favourite for the Hennessy at Newbury but fell two strides after the fourteenth fence when going easily.

High Edge Grey was a great favourite of Ken's and carried Ken's grand-daughter, Sandy Forster, to victory in a valuable Amateur Riders Handicap Chase at Kelso in February 1991, on her first ride under Rules Proper.

In all High Edge Grey won eight chases and was placed on fourteen occasions. His total prize money was nearly £50,000.

MERIDIAN II
Bay Gelding.
1967.
By Midlander-Steriolette.
A workmanlike type of horse who won seven chases including the Fred Withington over four miles at Cheltenham on 1st January, 1974.

It is worth noting that when Pappageno's Cottage was winning this important stayers race, it was run about the 8th or 9th January, but for the last twenty or so years has been one of the features of Cheltenham's enjoyable New Year meeting. Many people find this meeting and the May Hunter Chase meeting more enjoyable than the National Hunt Festival, due to the crowds the latter now attracts.

MOIDORE'S TOKEN
Bay Gelding.
1957.
By Moidore-Steel Token.
A great big horse who had been show-jumped before he arrived at Hassendean Bank. The owner, Pat Harrower, would virtually give Ken heart attacks when they went hunting together, as she would jump every-

thing in sight, including wire fences. In all Moidore's Token won nine chases, but very much his best race was in the 1968 Grand National, when he finished second to Red Alligator.

PAPPAGENO'S COTTAGE
Chestnut Gelding.
1955.
By Pappageno II-Dawn Cottage.
A very useful staying chaser who won one hurdle and ten chases, including the 1963 Scottish Grand National at Bogside. He also won the Fred Withington Chase, at Cheltenham in 1964 and 1965.

In the 1964 Grand National he was set to carry 11st. and started one of four joint favourites along with Time, Laffy and Flying Wild at 100-7. He finished tenth, ridden by Pat Taaffe. Time was a Willie Stephenson horse so named as he used to say, with his slight stutter, "H-h-he n-n-needs all the t-t-time in the world". The winner of the race was Team Spirit, ridden by Willie Robinson and trained by Fulke Walwyn, who got home by half a length from Purple Silk in one of the most exciting finishes since the war.

Pappageno's Cottage used to run in blinkers as although he was very genuine he liked to look around him in races. As Rhona says, "he would ask the other horses what they had for breakfast." Known as 'Old Pappa' in the yard he was a great favourite with everyone.

PRIZE CREW
Bay Gelding.
1962.
By Cash and Courage-Frigate Coming.
A very fast horse who won on thirteen occasions - one hurdle and twelve chases. The majority of times were over the minimum distance of two miles. A Wetherby specialist he won eight chases there.

RAMBLING JACK
Chestnut Gelding.
1971.
By Wreakin Rambler-Gilliana.
Very much Rambling Jack's best season was 1977/1978 when he won five chases including the valuable Ladbroke Trophy at Newcastle on 14th January over three and three quarter miles. His next race was the Greenall Whitley at Haydock when he was leading at the last, only to fall.

179

He was strongly fancied for the 1982 Grand National at 16/1 but fell at the first. He broke down in the 1982 Scottish Grand National and was retired. Rhona says of him, "He had a lovely retirement. He was ridden by his owner's wife and has only just died".

ROARING TWENTIES
Chestnut Gelding.
1960.
By Roaring Forties-Secret Pact.
Originally trained by Harry Bell, Roaring Twenties was transferred to the Olivers when Bell lost his licence for the first time.

His biggest win from Hassendean Bank was at the 1964 National Hunt Festival at Cheltenham when he won the County Hurdle ridden by George Milburn.

THE SPANIARD
Bay Gelding.
1962.
By Sayarijo-Perle d'Espagne.
One of the best horses ever to be stabled at Hassendean Bank. He was very atypical as he was not a chasing bred horse and had won three flat races before going to be trained by Ken. He was not a natural jumper and in fact George Milburn said of The Spaniard, having schooled him one day, "This horse will never jump, but he will always get to the other side".

Right until the end of his days he was liable to drop his shoulder, spin round and leave his surprised rider on the ground. This did not make him popular with his lad, but made the day for the rest.

The Spaniard was a very good juvenile hurdler, winning the important Lancashire Four Year Old Hurdle Meeting at Liverpool in March 1966 at the Grand National. Very much his best season was 1967/68 when he won six hurdles on the trot, including the George Duller at the Cheltenham Festival Meeting carrying 12st. 2lbs. He ran a particularly game race that day as he was giving at least 7 lbs. to all the other runners.

The next season he went chasing, winning three of his last four races including the Scottish Grand National in April 1970. While with the Olivers The Spaniard won a total of nineteen races - thirteen over hurdles and six chases.

His owner, a Mr. Rimmer, was obsessed with the horse and would constantly telephone to find out how his horse was - the record for telephone calls was nine in one day.

Ken did not want to run him in the 1971 Scottish Grand National as the going was far too firm for him. Mr. Rimmer insisted that The Spaniard ran and when he fell, removed the horse the following day and sent him to be trained elsewhere.

THREE TO ONE
Chestnut Gelding.
1971.
By Even Money-Yukon Girl.

Three To One was a useful staying chaser. He won six races over fences and all of his wins were over three or more miles. He was owned in partnership between Mr. Jimmy Manners and Rhona Oliver.

He was fancied for three Grand Nationals. In 1980 he started at 25-1 and fell at Bechers second time round, ridden by Mr. Geordie Dunn who later turned professional. The race was won by Ben Nevis and only four horses completed the course.

The next year he started at 33-1 and ran one of the best races of his career when he was fourth in the race which was won by Aldaniti. In 1982 he was joint third favourite with Aldaniti at 12-1, but fell at the first fence as did Rambling Jack.

Probably Three To One's best race was the 1982 Scottish Grand National when ridden by Jonjo O'Neill he was just beaten by the Ken Oliver trained winner, Cockle Strand.

TOM MORGAN
Chestnut Gelding.
1960.
By Canisbay-More Gold.

A useful chaser, Tom Morgan won four hurdle races between November, 1973 and March, 1974, before being sent chasing. In his first season's chasing, 1974/75, he won five races including the Mildmay Chase at that year's Grand National Meeting. The following season he won at the Cheltenham Festival Meeting in the National Hunt Two Mile Champion Chase.

However he made amends at the Festival the following year and on 14th March, 1977 he won the Grand Annual over two miles carrying 11st. 6lbs. when ridden by Tommy Stack, who is now a close friend of the Olivers. All in all he was a useful horse, winning on thirteen occasions - four hurdles and nine chases, which included the Mildmay and the Grand Annual.

TREGARRON
Bay Gelding.
1967.
By Never Say Die-Impudent.
Very much the joker in the pack as far as the other horses were concerned he had a top class, flat pedigree, as his dam Impudent had won an Oaks Trial at Lingfield and his sire, Never Say Die, the Derby itself.

He was bought very cheaply at Doncaster Sales after being spun by the vet as his hocks were not a true pair, but he proved himself a useful chaser winning seventeen over the bigger obstacles and one hurdle race.

Tregarron won on many of the Northern tracks including Ayr, Teeside, Kelso, Catterick, Hexham, Wetherby and a number of times at Haydock. Undoubtedly the best race he ran was in March 1973 when ridden by Colin Tinkler he won the Greenall Whitley over three miles at the latter course.

WYNDBURGH
Bay Gelding.
1960.
By Marquis-Swinnie.
A winner of thirteen races, all over fences, Wyndburgh was a great Aintree specialist. He won the important Eider Chase over 4¼ miles at Newcastle twice although the first time he won the race it was known as the Tote Investors Chase. His other two biggest wins were the Grand Sefton in 1957 and the Christmas Cracker Chase in December 1959.

He is one of the few horses to run in six consecutive Grand Nationals and on three occasions he was second, fourth once, sixth once and unseated his jockey at Bechers once. One of the four truly unlucky losers of the race since the turn of the century.

Wynburgh's career is covered in detail in the chapter 6, which is devoted mainly to him.

YOUNG ASHLEAF
Bay Mare.
1964.
By New Brigg-Yanny Ashdrop
Young Ashleaf was very much the best race mare ever to be stabled at Hassendean Bank, although we must not forget that Ken's line, which started with Sanvina, produced some top class brood mares.

Young Ashleaf won on the flat when trained by Ernie Weymess and

182

was sent to the Olivers in the middle of the 1967/68 season to run under National Hunt Rules. She won her first race at Newcastle and her last race at Doncaster that season.

In the 1968/69 season she only ran twice, winning over three miles on the hard at Cheltenham. The next season she ran eight times, winning on three occasions, and falling three times.

In 1970/71 Young Ashleaf was undoubtedly the best staying mare in the country over fences. She won the Scottish Grand National on 17th April and followed this up exactly seven days later by running second in the Whitbread.

Young Ashleaf had a very good season the next year, starting off by winning races at Carlisle and Doncaster and running second in late November, 1971 in the Hennessy at Newbury. In March she won the valuable Greenall Whitley chase over three miles at Haydock and her final win was in the Gordon Foster Chase, once again over three miles, in May 1972 at Wetherby.

A very good mare over fences, winning ten chases in all and being second in a Hennessy and Whitbread. She also ran creditably in the autumn of 1970 in the Colonial Cup run at Camden in the United States.